ONLY PARENT

Books by Louise Dickinson Rich

WE TOOK TO THE WOODS

HAPPY THE LAND

START OF THE TRAIL

MY NECK OF THE WOODS

TRAIL TO THE NORTH

ONLY PARENT

ONLY PARENT

Louise Dickinson Rich

Illustrated by Euclid Shook

PEOPLES BOOK CLUB
CHICAGO

PRINTED IN THE
UNITED STATES OF AMERICA

This is a special edition published exclusively for the members of THE PEOPLES BOOK CLUB, P.O. BOX 6570A, Chicago 80, Illinois, and 25 Hollinger Road, Toronto 13, Ontario, Canada. It was originally published by J. B. Lippincott Company.

Library of Congress Catalog Card Number 53-5416

CONTENTS

ILLUSTRATIONS

ONLY
PARENT

CHAPTER ONE

As It Was

"IF only he hadn't known the Popo Agie!" I read that the other day in "The Way West," a very good book by A. B. Guthrie, and it struck a responsive chord in my heart. The mountain man of the book would have been able to settle down in his later years, if only he hadn't in his youth lived for a time on the wild and beautiful river, the Popo Agie. If only we hadn't known the Rapid River! Then perhaps we, too, would have been able to accept and enjoy the conventional life of our day and age, the life of commuters' trains, and Country Club memberships, of rumpus rooms in the basement, and a quiet and desperate struggle to acquire for me a mink coat that would compare favorably with those of my Bridge Club associates. But we had known the Rapid River, and everything else thereafter was second-best.

The Rapid River runs southwest between two of the Rangeley Lakes, in the northwest corner of Maine. It is not navigable, being about the swiftest river east of the Rockies; it drops a hundred and eighty feet in three miles, with no falls, which is some kind of a record. And I will contend against all comers that it is the most beautiful river in the world. I have not seen all, or even very many, of the world's most famous rivers, but I've seen a lot of pictures of them, and I've talked with a lot of people who are more widely traveled than I am. I have yet to learn anything that will change my opinion.

The Rapid River comes tumbling down over descending ledges, and boiling around huge boulders left by the great glacier, filling the air with a deep, fluctuating roar. To me, the two loveliest sounds on earth are the sounds of water washing over stone, and of wind in the tops of trees. The rooms of our home, Forest Lodge, on Rapid River, are always full of them. I guess we never hear them, until we go away. Then we are suddenly aware that something is wrong, that the world seems suddenly stale and dull.

At intervals, the river levels off briefly into small pools, where the water runs still and deep, catching its breath for the next plunge into the rapids. None of the pools are alike, and they are all beautiful: Lower Dam Pool, the largest of them all, big enough so that you need a boat to fish it properly; Long Pool, with the sand-bar running out into it, making it an ideal place for the very young, or the inexpert, to swim; Smooth Ledge, which drops off steeply into deep water, so that you can dive from the rocks; and our own pool, which has no name except That Pool By Riches' Back Door, which is one of the nicest of them all, being deep and swirling, so that if you get caught in the current, the back-eddy will return you safely to the ramshackle float we knocked together out of abandoned boom-logs and weather-worn planks that had been jettisoned during dam repairs.

To me, the two loveliest sounds on earth are the sounds of water washing over stone, and of wind in the tops of trees. The rooms of our home, Forest Lodge, on Rapid River, are always full of them.

The banks of the river rise steeply on either side in ridges covered with pine and fir and spruce, interspersed with maple and birch. Except for us, nobody lives on them. Or at least, nobody lives there except the deer and the bear and the foxes, who come down in the dusk to drink, and the white-throated sparrows and partridges and thrushes. The partridges don't sing at all. The thrushes give concerts in the arrowy light of the setting sun, concerts of heart-breaking beauty. But the white-throated sparrows sing any old time they feel like it. It's wonderful to wake up in the middle of the night, when everything is black and still, and to hear that gay little flutey tune drifting through the darkness.

The whole world of lake and river and forest is cut off from the "civilized" world by a wall of mountains, through which one narrow, rough, and tortuous road winds along a bawling brook and through a slit of a pass to Andover, the nearest post-office. Andover is the beginning of what we call the Outside, meaning the world outside our own great, lofty, bowl-shaped plateau, the Inside. If this makes us sound like prisoners, I can only say that such an impression is wrong. If any of the eleven year-'round residents must, for some business or social reason, go Out, he groans and complains about the necessity for days in advance. Once Out, he rushes through his affairs, in order to get back In as soon as possible. It's the Inside that connotes freedom, and the Outside the restrictions of formal clothes, conventional manners, and walking on sidewalks. Probably the Outsiders pity us for being locked away in isolation behind the hills. We pity them because they are locked out of our special, secret world.

Ralph had known the Rapid River ever since he was a

child, when he spent his summers at the fishing camp at Middle Dam, run by Captain Coburn then, now owned by my friends, Larry and Alys Parsons. From the age of twelve, he'd vacationed there under the wing of old Mr. Wizwell, a dearly loved master at his school, Noble and Greenough. Since his mother expected a weekly letter from him during this annual interlude, and since he knew he'd never have time to write her during the summer, busy as he would be with fishing and collecting snakes and building tree huts, he devoted his study periods during the winter to writing the vague sort of letters that any mother knows she'll get from her son at summer camp. To wit: "Dear Mother, i am fine and having fun. The Fishing is good." (This would taper off into fair, tough, and no good, as the season went on and the water warmed.) "Could you send me a dollar?" (This was always a safe bet.) "i want to buy some Nick Carters. i caught a salmon. You're loving son, RALPH." He'd had the foresight to provide himself with camp stationery the season before, so all he had to do was stick a stamp over the pencilled sequence number that he had prudently inscribed, and drop it in the mail on Sunday. If a real emergency arose, he'd write an honest-to-God letter, much as it pained him. Maybe I shouldn't be handing on this device to other sons; but with him it worked, and it gave him more time to fall truly in love with the place.

Then, when he was grown, he bought Forest Lodge, a tumble-down place on the river, with the idea in mind that he would retire there some day. The day came simultaneously with the day that my sister and I and a group of assorted "sports," as we call them in Maine, were ending a three day canoe trip. We were straggling up the

Carry Road, under the auspices of John Lavorgna, the best guide I know, and I know a lot of them, when we drew abreast of a camp in need of a paint job. There was a man out in the yard, splitting wood, and we paused to pass the time of day.

I don't suppose that Ralph and I really looked at each other and burst into delighted laughter, but that is the way it seems to me now. At any rate, within six months we were married, and I, also, had come to live on the Rapid River. The general theme of our married life was that we did a lot of laughing, along with a lot of hard work. We didn't mind the work. You don't mind working if you can laugh, and Ralph and I amused each other like crazy. Neither of us was very funny, to other people; but we liked each other's brand of humor, and that was what counted.

If only we had never known the Rapid River! But we had, and so our whole lives were altered; and the first thing to be affected was domestic economy. We didn't need much money to live in the woods, but we did need some. In order to get it, we had to rearrange the conventional division of labor of the conventional American family, where Daddy goes to the office or factory and earns the money, and Mommy stays home and runs the house and takes care of the children. I discovered quite by accident that I could write stuff that people would buy, a fact that continues to surprise me. Ralph discovered that he could cook and liked messing around in a kitchen. So Ralph did part of the housework and cooking, while I wrote. Afternoons, I finished up where he'd left off, and he did his own outdoor work and picked up a little extra cash taxi-ing river-drivers or fishermen or lumberjacks or campers up and down the Carry Road. After Rufus was born, we split up the baby-sitting, too, the one taking over who could do it more conveniently at the moment.

Ralph was quite a baby-sitter. He started on his career as such sixty seconds after Rufus was born. I won't go into that affair in detail. Let me just state that I didn't get to the hospital as planned, no doctor could get into Forest Lodge in the middle of a blizzardy December night, so we simply let nature take its course. Or rather, nature took its course without bothering to ascertain our views on the subject. The baby turned out to be a healthy specimen, and his father snatched him up, and, disregarding my instructions to wash him and wrap him up warmly, held him up by the heels and greased him with some olive oil that he had stored away for the making of dry-fly dope, come spring. He looked exactly as though he were greasing a piston, and I gave a howl of anguish. But he said he'd read somewhere that you didn't wash babies any more. The modern procedure was to grease them; and it seems that he was right.

The next thing that he did to that defenseless child was to name him after a parrot. When Ralph was a boy, he'd had a Barbados parrot named Rufus, and he'd told me, even before we were married, that he was going to name his first son after that bird. He loved Rufus the Parrot, birds being one of the few pets available to an hotel-raised child. I thought he was making conversation, but it developed that he was serious, and right then I didn't feel up to a long argument. By the time I'd marshalled my forces, it was too late. The name had stuck. Anyhow, I'd discovered something even worse that he was doing to his son and heir.

He had decided that it was not at all necessary for babies to cry, except at stated times. Rufus could cry from five to six in the evening, but at no other times, unless there was something to cry about, like hunger or a safety pin sticking into him. So the minute he opened his little yap, Ralph clamped a hand over his nose and mouth. I was horrified when I found out, but Ralph said that was what the Indians did to their babies. An Indian couldn't afford to have a baby's squalling give away his position to hostile warriors; and if Indian babies could be taught by that method, so, by gosh, could Rufus. And what was more, he was not going to have his home-life ruined by a lot of tip-toeing around and "Sshh-the-baby's-asleep!"-ing. There was no need of it, he said. Let the kid get used to sleeping in a boiler factory, if necessary, and the sooner the quicker.

The odd thing about all this is that it worked, in spite of my fears. Rufus was the best baby I ever saw (make your own discount for maternal pride), almost never crying and possessing the ability to sleep like a log through a tornado, which is what our menage often resembled.

A year or so ago I was very much startled to have reported to me that my daughter Dinah had told a group of guests at the summer hotel at Middle Dam that she had been born in a paddy wagon, while her mother was on the way to jail. May I say hastily that there isn't a word of truth in this? She was born quite conventionally in a hospital, although I did have to call the police prowl car to get me there in time. I'll never forget those two nervous officers, asking every forty seconds as we flew over the icy road at sixty miles an hour, "Think you're goin' to make it, lady?" I made it, walking in and registering under my own power. But I understand why Dinah told that tale. She simply decided that it was time she had some attention, too, and if having been born under odd circumstances would get it for her—well, while she was at it, she might as well make it but *good.*

She was not named *for* Dinah Shore, just to clear the record. She was named *because* of Dinah Shore, who was pretty new at the time. I wanted to name her Elizabeth and Ralph wanted to name her Anne. I said they'd call her Annie, which I don't like, and he countered by asking how I'd like to have her called Lizzie. This was stalemate. We sat glowering at each other. Just then that old program, "The Chamber Music Society of Lower Basin Street," signed on, with Dinah Shore as soloist. We looked at each other and said, "Dinah. That's a good name. Not Diane. Dinah." Then we laughed. We didn't like to be mad at each other, ever. So Dinah is Dinah, with no middle name. She can take care of that later.

Living in the woods as we did, forty difficult miles away from the nearest doctor, we had to fall back on common sense to dictate proper procedure in the feeding, care, and training of the young. Oh, I had a little book, of course, but it had a disconcerting and unhelpful way of passing the buck every page or two by saying, "Consult your pediatrician." Consult my pediatrician, indeed! I didn't even know where there was one. Probably no nearer than Portland, which was too far away to be at all practical. But we had raised a lot of pups, kittens, and assorted wild life, so we developed and applied the theory that babies, too, are just young animals, and whatever is OK for a puppy is OK for a small child. My Sargeant's book on dog-care was a lot more help to me than my baby-care book. At least Mr. Sargeant realized that most people weren't going to high-tail it to the nearest vet every time a puppy sneezed. I had to modify some of his pronouncements slightly on some occasions, but we came out all right in the long run.

Ralph had an odd idea of songs suitable for lullabies, not that our children ever had need of lullabies. They dropped like poled oxen when it was time for them to go to sleep. Lullabies were more of a form of entertainment that we furnished for them; or at least, Ralph did, since he could sing and I cannot. At one time he had known eighty singing limericks, suitable for stag nights, of which he could recall about forty. I suppose I should be thankful that the other forty had been lost in limbo. The only song that he sang Rufus that I even half-way approved of was the Virginia Hunt Club Song, which goes something like, "Drink, puppy, drink, Let every puppy drink, Who's old enough to gape and to swallow." So far, so good; but it goes on, "We are riding to the hounds, So pass the bottle 'round, And merrily we'll whoop and we'll holloa." I made a point of handing to Rufus his bottle of formula during this song, whenever possible, to establish the right association in his unformed mind.

Since something had to be done to counteract this evil influence, and since I can't sing, I took to reciting poetry to the baby as he played in his pen while I did the dishes or baked bread. It was my opinion that babies don't understand what you're saying anyhow, that all they are interested in is the sound of a human voice, flowing quietly and rhythmically along. So, with my hands mittened in bread dough, I would announce, "The world is too much with us. Late and soon, Getting and spending we lay waste our powers." Or I'd warn, "Do not brood overlong on angels Should a fearful and uncertain king, Direct your path. To be confused With angels in a world unused to rapture Is a dangerous thing." Or I'd declaim, "I have fallen in love with American names, The sharp names that never get fat." And I'd roll them over my tongue, Medicine Hat, Tucson, Deadwood, Painted Post, Pretty Prairie, Middle Dam, and Nantucket. The baby would sit looking at me solemnly, with wide brown eyes, and then say, "Goo!"

I don't think early conditioning amounts to much, informed opinion to the contrary. If it did, Rufus would love fooling around with words. Actually he considers reading and writing fit only for girls, invalids, and sissies. He prefers action, violent if possible. He had his indoctrination at the age of four, when we were all visiting his grandparents in Bridgewater, Massachusetts, for Thanksgiving. I heard the fire alarm sound, and a few minutes later saw the car of a neighbor go whizzing up the street with a mess of kids, Rufus among them, in back. They didn't return for a long, long time, but I didn't worry, because I was sure that they had gone to the fire, and that Mr. Colby would take good care of Rufus. When he finally did come back, he ran into the house with his eyes bugging.

And this is the story that he had to tell. They'd all gone to a big building with smoke pouring out of the windows and some men on the roof shooting other men. The men on the roof threw a dead man off. Then the fire department came and some of the firemen put out the fire and the rest turned hose on the bad men, and pretty soon some soldiers came and started shooting, too, and they threw some bombs, and the men on the roof started crying and some other men in uniform came and took them away.

Now what do *you* make of that? I made of it that Rufus understood more of the Crime Does Not Pay programs that his father doted on than I had realized, and I said, "Now wait a minute, Rufus. You know nothing like that really happened. People don't act that way, except on the radio." He'd never been to the movies, so for once I couldn't blame *them*. "Now tell me what really happened."

His eyes popped wider than ever. "It *did* happen! Honest, Ma."

Just then the radio switched from a musical program on to a news broadcast, and the news was that the prisoners at the State Farm, outside Bridgewater, had staged a riot, burning their bedding in their cells, overpowering two guards and taking their guns, killing at least one, and taking refuge on the roof. They had finally been subdued by the fire department and troops called from Camp Edwards, who had used tear gas to bring them under control. Period.

I apologized to Rufus. His report had been as accurate as his limited experience and vocabulary would permit. That day started his career of managing always to be on the scene of the crime. He's covered fires, grade crossing accidents, and the Lord only knows what-all. He had a really big evening last fall (we are back in Massachusetts now). First he went to the Public Library to return a book for me. Just as he was coming out, he saw a car hit an old man who was trying to cross the street, and he stayed there until the victim was removed to the hospital. (He later was able to tell me the man's name and the name of the hospital.) Then he drifted over past the Town Hall and jail, and he heard someone inside the jail hollering, as he called it. Rufus hollered back, and the man informed him that it was all a terrible mistake, he was a respectable citizen, locked up for no good reason, and would Rufus immediately go get him a lawyer. Rufus said, "Sure, sure, take it easy."

"And did you?" I asked in some horror, since I knew our family lawyer wouldn't relish being dragged out on a Saturday evening.

Rufus looked disgusted. "Naw, of course not. He was just a drunk. The cops would have got him a lawyer if they wanted him to have one." Anyhow—

He then took a reconnoitering trip around town on his bike—kids can cover an awful lot of territory on a bike—arriving at a cross-roads just after a convertible had gone off the pike and turned over twice, to the detriment of the physical well-being of the four occupants. He stayed until that mess was more or less cleaned up, and then came home. I asked him why he'd come home so early, what with one thing and another.

"Aw, there wasn't anything interesting to do," he told me, and went into his room to listen to something really exciting, like *The Mystery Theater* or *Suspense*. He should be valuable to some newspaper; but since the age of three his one love has been motors of all sorts. My whole married life was spent with one man whom I suspected of valuing an old Packard more than he did me; and I have a feeling that my life as the only parent of another male is going to follow the same pattern.

When I discovered that I was going to have a second

child, Ralph informed me that, if I could conveniently arrange it, he'd like another boy. I didn't care much one way or the other. My attitude was that you took what you got and liked it. Yes, Ralph said, but boys are easier than girls. You know where you stand with boys. With boys you say, "Look, son, this is how it's going to be, or how'd you like a poke in the jaw?" That fixes things up fine, with no misunderstandings or hurt feelings on either side. But with girls—

"Yeah?" I said. "And what about with girls?" I don't think he liked the way I said it.

"Now don't take this personally," he begged, "but with girls, if you say a thing like that, where do you end up? With hurt feelings and sulks and tears, and you don't know where you're at, except that you're probably in the wrong. With girls you have to fool around being tactful and cagey, and I haven't got the time for that bushwah. *Nor* the patience. I'm telling you right now, if this is a girl, it's *your* baby. I wash my hands of the whole affair."

That worried me some. I didn't want a little girl whose father was going to break her heart by ignoring her, a little girl who would try and try to please, and get nowhere with it. I'd seen children like that.

To me all small babies look alike, and they're all homely; but Dinah was even homelier than that. She was red and wrinkled and skinny. She looked like a starved little ape, and I did not anticipate with any great glee her father's first viewing of her. I'd have liked to have had a chance to fatten her up some before he saw her, but that was out of the question. I did make a semi-apology for her appearance, but before I could launch into my promises for better things to come, Ralph interrupted me.

"Why, she is *not* ugly!" he announced belligerently. "She has a very pretty mouth." Well, come to look more closely, so she did. So! *That's* the way it was going to be! I relaxed all over.

Then came the day when I brought the new baby in to Forest Lodge. I got off the boat at Middle Dam, and sat down on the porch with her in my arms, waiting for the mail to be sorted so I could go home. Behind me, through the open window, I could hear Ralph talking to Alys Parsons. "Come on. You can leave the mail for a minute. Come see my new daughter."

Al was very good-natured about it. She dropped what she was doing and came out to inspect the wizened little face which was all she could see of the swaddled infant. "Umhum," she said. "Frankly, she looks just like any other new baby." Al is honest. I burst into hoots of laughter, because that's what I thought, too; but Ralph took umbrage. She was *not* like any other baby, and if Al and I were so stupid and lacking in vision as to think that she was, so much the worse for us! For a man who didn't want a baby girl, who would have nothing to do with such a project, he put on quite an act.

For two years after that, we had a wonderful time. I guess it was because we all loved and enjoyed each other and didn't give a continental about much else. Both kids could swim as soon as they could walk, because in a country composed of almost as much water as land, to save yourself worry, you teach your young to swim early. Then if they fall into a river or lake—as they inevitably will, time and again—they can get themselves out. When you miss a child for five minutes, you don't go into hysterics, picturing them drowned. So, from June through October, we all went swimming every afternoon. On the Fourth of July, I did my annual dive. I *hate* going into the water head-first, preferring to inch in—the hard way, so they tell me; but to prove that I can, I dive once a year. This is sort of a boat-drill, to keep me fit for an emergency. My July dive was always a cause for celebration. All the rest of the family would plunge in after me, Dinah included. They'd swim in circles around me and do surface dives, *à la* the porpoise, coming up on the other side of this old tug-boat, with the intention of making me feel ashamed of my chicken attitude.

Then we had a mess of pets, dogs, cats, rabbits, a raccoon, and a skunk, to say nothing of the bantams and the mink that lived in the foundation of the chimney, and who is the nearest I have come to date to that mink coat. We all enjoyed them and failed to keep them in their places. Rufus used to take the skunk to bed with him, and Dinah cherished a bunny. I did all my housework with a sea of Siberian huskies milling around my knees. We just loved animals, that's all.

We had as much fun working together as we did playing together. Rufus helped his father on the various motors we'd become possessed of, putting his little hand into a space too narrow for Ralph's big paw to turn a bolt or retrieve a nut. Dinah, still a toddler, filled the cats' saucers with canned milk or dusted the rungs of the chairs. We had no money. We dressed in the most disreputable clothes, and we ate the simplest foods. We had no entertainment, except each other, and we had a marvelous life.

Then it ended. Between one minute and the next, Ralph suffered a cerebral hemorrhage. One minute he was laughing with me, then he gave a sigh, then he was dead. I now realize what a wonderful thing it was to have happened. He might have made a partial recovery, and been crippled and paralyzed in a wheel chair. He couldn't have borne that. Life without action would have been hell for him. I'm glad, now, that he was so lucky. But after the shock and the grief of the moment had passed, I realized only one thing: that I was alone now and that for all the rest of my life I was going to be lonely; that from now on in, I was an Only Parent.

CHAPTER TWO

Only Parenthood

THERE has been a great deal of talk and head-shaking about the lot of the Only Child, and I guess some of it is well-founded. Presumably where there's smoke, there's fire. But this is a matter I am ill qualified to discuss. My own career as an only child was very brief, and I have little remembrance of it. My mother cleverly arranged to have her second baby on my second birthday, which also happens to be Flag Day, the 14th of June; so that for years my sister and I had an exaggerated opinion of our own importance. The birthdays of other children of our acquaintance might come and go with only family recognition, but for the little Dickinson girls everyone who owned a flag broke it out and set it flying. I don't remember when or how we became disabused of this idea.

But I do remember the day that my sister was born, although everyone tells me that that is impossible, that nobody can remember things that happened when she was just exactly two. I do, though. My father took me out into the yard and told me that I was going to have a wonderful birthday present, something alive and cute. At the time we were living in the Berkshires, and I remember standing near the bee-hives with my hand in his, looking down into the beautiful valley below and thinking to myself that it would surely be a puppy, which I wanted more than anything in the world.

It turned out to be Alice, just a red, squally baby; and I am sorry to report that I was not at all nice about it. I used to sneak up to her carriage when no one was looking and pinch her and pull horrible faces at her to make her cry, poor little thing. I thought that if she made enough of a nuisance of herself, my mother would give her away. Fool that I was; because on the contrary everyone paid much more attention to her than they did to me, and I overheard my Aunt Maud say to my mother, "I guess Someone's nose is out of joint." Children aren't so stupid, and I knew from the tone that the Someone was me. Thereafter, for quite a while, I lived in terror and seized every possible opportunity to study my nose in a mirror, watching and waiting for it to turn from an undistinguished, but at least inoffensive, snub button into a repulsive monstrosity. Alice would be to blame, I reasoned dimly, and if, on top of not being a puppy, she did that to me—Well, I wouldn't be responsible for the consequences.

However, in a few years we became extremely good friends, and grew up having a lot of fun together. To this day, I have a better time with Alice than I do with anyone else. She has the zany, glancing sort of wit that reduces me to a giggling jelly. But all that is beside the point. The point was that I have had little experience in being an only child.

Only Parenthood

I've had a lot of experience as an Only Parent, and it seems to me that this odd species deserves as much attention as the Genus Only Child. There must be quite a few of us kicking around, but nobody pays much attention to us and our problems.

People who talk constantly about their wonderful and exceptional children both bore and irritate me. Most children, in my experience—and I used to be a school-teacher, so have known quite a few—are cattle of much the same color, and this includes my own two. I hope I will not be misunderstood. I love my children and enjoy them no end. I can see, however, that they might conceivably not be quite as fascinating to other people as they are to me. So I am not going to talk about them in panegyric terms. But I'll have to talk about them some, since you can't be left a widow with children aged seven and two without their influencing your life enormously. Influencing, did I say? That's this week's understatement. For the past eight years, since the sudden and tragic death of my husband, my life has been completely shaped by the fact that I have had two small children to support and bring up. I don't know what I would have been doing during those eight years if I'd been childless, but I do know that it wouldn't have been any of the things that I've found myself doing. I might have taken a trip around the world. I might have joined the WAVES. I might have learned to fly, or raised Chinooks or orchids, or gone to live in the Channel Islands. I don't know. I do know that I wouldn't have spent much time in Bridgewater, Mass., or taken a cottage at the beach, or ever become expert at picking up snakes and stroking them into quiet. But more of all that later.

There are both advantages and disadvantages to being an only parent, as there are to any state of life to which any of us may be elected. To my mind, the disadvantages outweigh the advantages. The only good thing that I can see about it is that there is no possible split in policy. There is no having the buck passed to you in a ticklish situation with the elaborately off-hand remark, "Go ask your mother"; no chance to play the coward with the threat, "Just wait until your father gets home and I tell him about *this!*" I hope I wouldn't ever have said that anyhow, but there's no telling to what depths I might have sunk, if I were tired and irritated enough. As it is, I have to stand on my own two feet as Authority. Probably it's good for my character.

The disadvantages are pretty obvious. First and foremost, of course, is that just as authority is not divided, so is responsibility not shared. If you make a mistake in judgment, and who doesn't once in a while, you alone are to blame. There is no one in the whole world to whom you can go for help, who will give his whole mind and heart to the problem, backed by an intimate knowledge of the mind and heart and body of the child. Only a parent has that, and there is no other parent. You have to go ahead alone, doing the best you can, and that sometimes turns out to be a poor best. I almost lost Rufus once, when he was eleven, because of a lapse on my part.

We were all at my mother's at the time. At about nine o'clock of a Sunday evening I decided that Rufus didn't look very chipper. Cross examination brought to light the fact that he had been feeling terrible all day, but hadn't told me because he thought—rightly—that I would make him go to bed, and he wanted to play baseball. I shoved

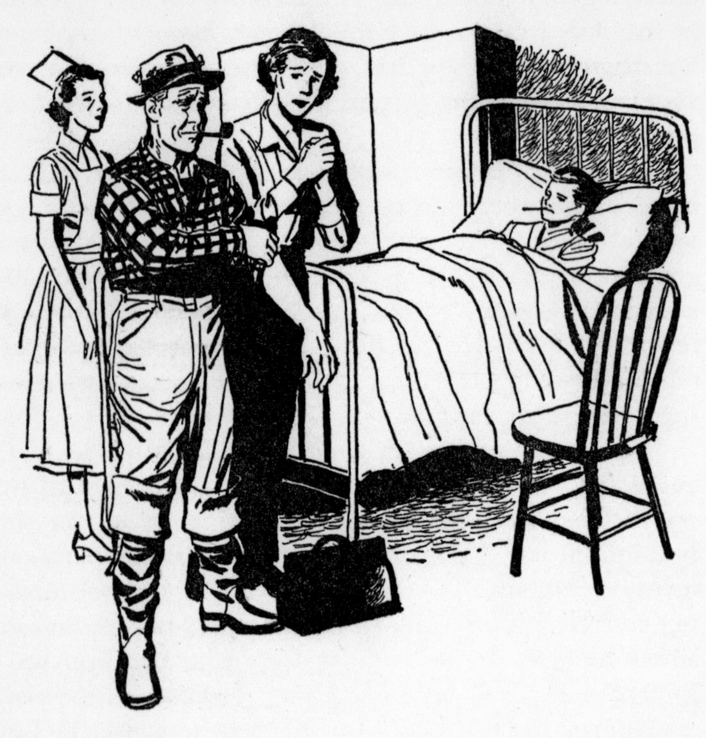

The surgeon arrived, and a less professional figure I never saw, dressed as he was in dungarees and hip boots, a plaid shirt and an old beat-up felt hat.

a thermometer into his mouth, found his temperature to be a neat 103, and discovered that his stomach ache had moved over into his right side. Much as I disapprove of bothering busy physicians on their only day off, if it can be avoided, I called the family doctor. He confirmed my lay diagnosis that this had all the appearance of acute appendicitis, and the sooner we got the boy to the hospital, the better.

The hospital is two towns away, and of course at that time of night there was no surgeon on duty. In fact, they were all away for the week-end. There was one who had gone fishing down on Cape Cod, and his wife thought possibly he'd be home by the time we got there. I threw a few things into a bag for Rufus, and the doctor and I set out for Brockton. By now, naturally, it had started raining harder than I ever saw it rain in my life.

The surgeon arrived at about the same time we did, and a less professional figure I never saw, dressed as he was in dungarees and hip boots, a plaid shirt and an old beat-up felt hat. I thought, "*That* character lay hand on my son? Only over my dead body!" But Rufus was turning an interesting purple color, and my poise was shaken additionally by the belated discovery that I had on bedroom slippers, into which I'd changed earlier in the evening to rest my feet. So I allowed them to whisk the kid away. After a while they came back to where I was sitting in the dim, deserted waiting-room, turning the pages of an old magazine, to say that they wanted a conference with me. I didn't recognize the surgeon at first. He'd changed into whites and was a different man. I apologized to him silently. They told me that it did indeed look like appendicitis, except for the presumably infallible test, the blood count. That was all wrong. It should be very high, and it was normal. What did I want them to do?

Now how would I be able to answer a question like that? I didn't want them slicing the poor kid up unnecessarily. I have always harbored a completely unjust suspicion that surgeons sit in their offices, grinning evilly and honing their knives and simply drooling for any slim excuse to use them. (I know; I said it was unjust.) On the other hand, I certainly wanted whatever was best for my son to be done. I brooded for five precious minutes, asking what I hoped sounded like intelligent questions, and then did the only intelligent thing. I said, "I don't know. Do what you think is best." It seemed that they thought it best to operate at once.

"When is at once?" I asked. "To-morrow morning?"

"To-morrow morning? No, right now, within ten minutes." So that is what they did, and a very good thing, too, as the appendix burst while they were taking it out and we had an awful time getting the kid back on his feet.

The moral of this tale is this: Six years before, our local Maine doctor told me that Rufus had a funny type of blood, low on white corpuscles. What was normal in anybody else was a high white count for him. In short, he was an infector. The matter had never come up again, so I had forgotten about it. I should have remembered and told the doctors, and saved the little time that might have made a lot of difference. If there had been two of us parents, one of us would probably have remembered. I might have myself, if I hadn't been so harassed with sole responsibility. Luckily the consequences were not fatal, but if they had been, I'd have been to blame.

Another disadvantage of this business is the twenty-four hour shift. The husbands of my friends take over once in a while and give their wives a break. They take their off-spring to the Rodeo or the Sportsman's Show, while their wives sit at home with their feet up, reading improving books and having a nice rest. That isn't how it works in my family! *I* take Rufus and Dinah to the Rodeo, and it is my personal opinion that if you have seen one cowboy fall off a horse, or one steer roped and thrown, you have seen them all. A whole afternoon of that sort of nonsense is too much of a good thing. And as for the Sportsman's Show—you can have it. I used to enjoy it in the olden days when I could see and do what I wanted to. I liked the State Exhibits, and the Moose Calling and Fly Casting Contests, and the boats. I liked drifting around and chatting with the guides and wardens whom I knew back home. But those days are gone, I guess forever.

The thing that interests me least in the world is a trailer. So what are my children most fascinated by at the Sportsman's Show? Trailers, of course. And will they be content to go through *one,* admiring the compact space-planning, looking into closets and refrigerators, turning on the shower-bath and jumping on the bunks to test the springs? Certainly not. They have to go through each and every one of them—by actual count, thirty-two—and *then* go back to check and compare various features. If I never see another trailer, it will be much too soon.

The Only Parent, I very well realize, can easily become the Over-cautious Parent, in an effort to guard herself against the inevitable grief and remorse that will follow a fatal mistake. That I do try to avoid, since I feel that children, even at the ages of fifteen and ten (as they now are), are entitled to some form of private life, to some freedom to learn about the world and the things and people who are in it, first-hand. The result, so my mother tells me, is that I am over-lenient. Maybe I am. I have no way of judging. I only know that my children seldom let me down, that children are capable of acting much more sensibly and adequately than is usually required of them. You grow only as big as is demanded of you, after all.

Then this business of trying to be a father and wage-earner as well as a mother and succorer does take a toll. I'd love to be all soft and feminine, a lily or an ivy plant, nourished and protected and adored. I'd love to have the responsibilities and problems of earning a living and making decisions and administering discipline and coping with the man who has come to fix the roof taken over by someone else, who would be better fitted to discuss tax declarations and copper flashings than I am. Then I could be all dimples, sweeping tea-gowns, and lady-like charm. Or at least I could give it a try. I could adorn and grace my home, rather than just be the old biddy who runs it and goes out to raise ructions with the telephone repair men who cut down one of my trees. But that isn't the way things are, so there's no sense in indulging in might-be's. I have to be mean and nasty and tough and hard, although those are qualities truly foreign to my nature. I realize with regret how much being an only parent has changed me for the worse.

Before Ralph died, we used to be what is known to the trade, I believe, as a Nice Little Family. There were Mommy, Daddy, Big Brother, and Little Sister. It was a very good and happy arrangement, which I recommend highly, with a few slight alterations. First, if I had it all to do over again—and if it were possible—I would not wait until I was in my thirties to start a family. It's too hard on the frame. I'm too old now to play *Run, Sheep, Run* and *Red Rover, Come Over* and *Duck On A Rock* without suffering repercussions, like shortness of breath, Charlie horses, and various bruises and contusions. If I'm in this sad condition now, think what I'll be by the time the kids are graduated from college, if they ever are. Lord, I'll be attending their Commencements in a wheel chair, brandishing an ear trumpet.

Second, I'd have my children closer together, if possible. Five years between children is too much, especially if they are not of the same sex. When you add to the natural sex barrier a barrier of age, you are cheating your children out of one of the most enjoyable relationships there is. I speak from my own childhood experience, when my sister and I had such a wonderful time together. My children could have a lot more fun with each other, if they were nearer of an age.

Sometimes, though, they surprise me very much. They may be in a fight to end all fights. (Do all siblings fight, I wonder?) They may be screaming at each other, and saying how much they hate each other, and spitting and slapping at each other like a couple of Kilkenny cats. Tears of sheer rage will be pouring down Dinah's cheeks as she uses some of the expressions she's picked up from the lumberjacks, which I deplore, and which don't sound very well on the lips of a little girl; and Rufus will be taunting her, calling her chicken for crying, and otherwise behaving in an objectionable manner. But if I try to interfere, or the kid from next door comes along and wants to make it a three-cornered fight, you'd be amazed at how quickly the breach is healed. Dinah moves over to stand beside her brother, her tears suddenly dry, her eyes narrowed and glinting dangerously, and what will some day be her bosom heaving in an ominous way. Rufus adopts a bull-necked, "Oh, yeah?" stance; and ordinarily they rout the foe without having to fire a single shot, so impressive is their solid front. They may then go right back to their own fight, but usually the spirit has gone out of it. I don't think I'm going to worry too much about their affection for each other.

They are, thank heaven, of diverse temperaments. I don't know whether I could survive two of either one of them. Dinah is a perfectionist, as her father was. She wants to do everything just exactly right, to get all A's on her report card, and to please her mother and teacher in everything. She's the type that would paint the inside of the storage space under the sink, which nobody would ever see, just for her own satisfaction in a job properly done. That is a very worthy attitude and one that I admire; but I feel sorry for the poor little girl. It is impossible for one person to be always right, always best in everything, and she's going to have some sad moments while she's discovering that.

Rufus is like me. To heck with the space under the sink! We can't be bothered with finnicking details, as long as the general effect is good. We deal in broad, sloppy gestures and sweeping and inaccurate generalizations, and all that we really want is peace. That is not a proper attitude, I am the first to admit, and every now and then I pull myself up short, swearing to do better. I never do, though.

The other day I had a very chastening experience. I

overheard a conversation between my off-spring. Dinah had gone to Rufus for sympathy, because I had spoken to her fairly sharply for not hanging up her coat when she came in. For yak-king at her, she called it. She was almost in tears and complaining bitterly about the cruel treatment she received at the hands of the old witch. (Me, she meant, but I could overlook that, since I was eavesdropping anyhow.)

Rufus said, in a slow, patient, and paternal manner, "Look, Dinah, why don't you do what I do? When Ma starts yammering at me, I just shut my ears and think of something else. I let it go in one ear and out the other. All you have to do is say *yes* and *no* once in a while. She doesn't know the difference. If she wants to rave, it doesn't hurt me, and it must do her some good, or she wouldn't bother."

I slunk away. How right he was. But I hadn't thought I was that transparent. I determined to mend my ways and not yak purely for my own satisfaction. Parenthood seems to involve a constant making of good resolutions, some of which I actually do keep.

Having been a parent for fifteen years, and an Only Parent for eight, I ought to be coming up with some profound and valuable thoughts on the subject. I'm sorry to say that the longer I play this game, the less I know about it. When I was an old-maid school-teacher, I was simply brimming over with ideas on how other people should bring up their children. I'd give advice at the drop of a hat, or even if I saw a hat that looked like dropping. Boy, I was full of theories! Good ones, too.

Now I am older and wiser, although not necessarily sadder. Now I know that there are no six simple rules for the successful rearing of a family, and that even if there were, by the time I'd mastered them my children would have grown into another phase, and they'd no longer apply. Children are growing individuals and should be treated as such, a program that involves no rules at all, but only an attempt at understanding. That's a pretty trite observation, but only experience can teach you how true it is.

There is just one big difference between children and other people, and it is the difference that makes them so enchanting. Children are not sophisticated; and after all, why should they be? They haven't been in the world long enough to have become worn and frayed and surfeited by it. Everything is new and fresh and full of delight for them. My children come home and tell me the most awful, corny jokes, jokes that were fatigued when I was in training pants; and that, believe me, was a long time ago. "Why does an Indian wear feathers in his hair?" (To keep his wig warm. Wigwam. Get it, Ma? Ha-ha-ha!) Or "What did one wall say to the other?" (Meet you at the corner. Pretty neat, huh, Ma?) I laugh genuinely, but not at the so-called joke. I laugh for joy that such simple things are still amusing even to the A-bomb age young.

Or they come in and say, "Hey, Ma, do you know about eggs hatching? Come quick. We've found a partridge nest, and the babies are just pecking to get out. We can't stay long. Their old lady is having a fit." So I run like mad, spend five minutes waiting for the little beaks to come through, and then retire at the behest of the children to let the little birds' own mother take over. She's a very handsome lady, although understandably nervous on this occasion, fluttering around and doing her broken-wing act to toll us away.

Or I will say, "Look, mutts, help me a minute. I need some extra hands to put the laundry away." (They know all about laundry. Rufus started and ran the gasoline-powered washing-machine for me, Dinah shook out the clothes as they fell from the wringer into the basket, and handed clothes-pins to me while I hung out, and we all took it in together.) "These sheets," I say, "have to go on the bottom of the pile in the linen closet. So you, Rufus, lift up the pile, and you, Dinah, slick out the wrinkles, and I'll shove these in under."

"Why?" they ask.

"So we can rotate them, and not be using the same old sheets over and over, while the others loaf."

"Gee, pretty clever!" they exclaim admiringly. "How'd you ever think that one up, Ma?" I refrain from explaining that I did not think it up. I grab credit from my young wherever I can find it. And I think it's reassuring that such simple matters are magic affairs to the young. When you're that age

> The angels keep their ancient places.
> Turn but a stone, and start a wing.
> 'Tis ye—'tis your estrangéd faces
> That miss the many-splendoured thing!

The world is admittedly in somewhat of a mess nowadays, but it should still be a beautiful and wonderful place for children. If it isn't in childhood, it never will be for all their lives; and then where goes our hope for the future? To achieve peace and contentment, to appreciate beauty and wonder, you must first recognize them through happy experience. It is up to the parent to provide that experience. The sometimes ugly stone of reality is there to be seen plainly. It's the parent's duty and privilege to help the child to turn the stone, or to see and recognize the starting wing, to acknowledge and love and make a part of his life the many-splendoured things of the natural world and the world of mind and spirit.

CHAPTER THREE

"Bring Your Friends Home, Dears . . .

SUDDENLY left with two small children to bring up, I had to fall back on the rules laid down by *Parents' Magazine* and similar publications, and on some of the lofty pronouncements that I, myself, had so blandly delivered to the distracted parents of various pupils of mine in the days when I was free, white, and well over twenty-one. Among others was the one that runs, "You should say, 'Bring your friends home, Dear, so that Mother can meet them.'" My kids took me at my word; and oh, boy, have my horizons been broadened!

I have met, through the good offices of my son, for example, an Indian chief, Chief Tall Horse. That isn't his name. I am not using his real name, because if he is still alive and in business, I don't want to queer his pitch. He really was an Indian, and he really was a chief; but his business was what I would call a racket. He traded on his race and status. He went about the country, showing up at resorts and sporting events, and usually received free board and lodging, to say nothing of honorariums, just for his atmosphere value. He had it good. He'd look noble and austere, and give out with bits of Indian lore in a sort of Indian dialect. He would even say, "Ugh, me no like," and the Out-of-State sports would be no-end impressed. Our paths crossed during a canoe meet on the Rapid River, and after he'd sat on my porch talking with Rufus and me for an hour or so, I realized that he could speak better English than I could. He was a nice-looking, clean old man, resembling the back of a buffalo nickel, and actually I guess I don't blame him too much for taking in all the traffic would bear, if he could get away with it. My one problem with him was what to call him. Chief? Mr. Horse? Hey, you? I never did decide.

A couple of years ago, Rufus came into the house in Maine with a dark young man in a beret, white silk ascot, and midnight-blue flannel jacket, whom he introduced as Douglas Martin, off the drive. He looked like no river-driver I'd ever seen. He was much too well-groomed and stylish; but I realized he'd probably dressed up to go calling. He, too, was an Indian, from one of the Canadian reservations, and his real name was something like Summit-in-the-Clouds. Since there was a labor shortage locally, the Company had imported some men under bond from across the Border, and Douglas was among them. I have never, anywhere, met anyone with such beautiful manners. He never failed to rise when I entered the room. He never failed to thank me for my hospitality when he left, even though he had to chase me way out to the clothes yard to do so, and even though he was in and out of the house almost daily, and my so-called hospitality seldom consisted of more than a bottle of Coke (which he had to get out of the refrigerator himself), and a fistful of icebox cookies. He was quick to see things to be done, like a heavy log to be put into the fire-place, or a banging shutter to be fastened. When the drive moved on, he made a point of walking four miles down to Forest Lodge and back to say good-bye. We old ladies appreciate this kind of attention. He was a very nice young man, but I know a lot of nice young men whose manners, through circumstance, are far from polished. I wondered about that, and I finally found the answer. Douglas had been educated and trained by the Sisters of the Order in charge of the school on his reservation. I'd like to take a few lessons from those Sisters, myself, in the teaching of deportment.

Then there was a teamster, Jerry Millis, who used to let the kids ride on the team with him, and finally hauled some wood for me in his spare time. He had as his constant companion the most beautiful, ugly, bow-legged English bull-dog I ever saw, one of those huge, bumbling creatures with over-shot jaws that look so mean and are so gentle. I don't know where Jerry got him. He should have been a show-dog, and not just bumming around the woods. Jerry used to amuse me no end. In any conversation that I ever had with him—and I had quite a few—he would eventually remark solemnly, "I always say there's *nothing* like a mother! That's what I always say, Miz Rich." Well, when you come right down to it, I suppose there is nothing, biologically, like a mother. And as far as his always saying so goes, he sure did, to me at least. Probably he was trying to make me feel important. There's nothing like a second cousin twice removed, either, and without doubt if Jerry had met one, he'd have always said that, too.

I learned from Jerry a good thing not to do, and I'll

pass it on, in case necessity or impulse should ever overtake you, which I most sincerely hope it won't. As is often the case in lumbercamp bar-rooms—and a bar-room in a lumbercamp is simply a bunkhouse, *nothing* else—the beds are often lousy, in the true sense. (In both senses, possibly.) This is unavoidable, with so many men, some of them with indifferent habits of cleanliness, drifting in and out. The same blankets are used continually, and of course there are no sheets or pillow cases. If you get assigned to a lousy bunk, you have to use your own methods to improve the situation, and the method Jerry used was rather drastic. He doused his bunk with kerosene. I guess this probably worked, as far as getting rid of the lice went; but as in many operations that are successful, the patient died—or pretty nearly. Jerry went to bed without airing the blankets and woke up in agony, burned from top to toe, not from flame, but from contact with the kerosene soaked bedding. The last I saw of him, they were removing him to a hospital. I didn't know before that such a thing was possible. I'm telling you, just in case you have lived as sheltered a life as I have, *beware!*

Of course, if Ralph had been alive, I would have had only a superficial acquaintance with Tall Horse and Douglas and Jerry. As man of the house and father of the son who had brought these friends home, he would have attended to the demands of hospitality to the occasional male visitor. Women in the wild country, where there is no electric power and therefore no handy labor saving devices such as electric lights and vacuum cleaners and automatic ovens, have too much to do keeping the house running to fritter time away sitting and talking at ten o'clock in the morning. While Ralph kept the company

When Rufus was about three years old he brought home a man who was working on the log drive, a river-hog, as we call them. And that is how I met Rush Rogers, who came in for an afternoon's call between booms, and stayed two years.

out of my hair and from under my feet, I would have been punching down my bread, or working on a short story, or washing kerosene lamp chimneys. But the Only Parent can't slope off about her own concerns, leaving the entertainment of guests to a small child who has neither the experience nor the conversational facility for the job. No, she has to leave her ironing to mildew in the basket while she does her poor best to sound intelligent on subjects concerning which she knows little or nothing.

Having drawn this pathetic picture of myself and—I hope—enlisted your sympathy, I will now come clean and admit that I learned an awful lot from these conversations; and anyhow, I'd rather talk than work any old day of the week.

Actually I used to go into my Bring-your-friends-home routine before Ralph died; and when Rufus was about three years old he brought home a man who was working on the log drive, a river-hog, as we call them. This man looked like all river-hogs, with stagged pants (stagged means hacked off just below the knee with any dull-edged cutting instrument, and unhemmed), and a two day stubble. I gave the pants a Look. There was something wrong with them. They were not Sears Roebuck. They were not what we call Monty Ward. (I was a specialist in both fields.) They were—well, I finally asked, in what I hoped was a friendly and inoffensive manner, "Where'd you get those pants?"

"Brooks Brothers," he told me, and turned down the waist band to show me the label. "They're some I had left over."

"Left over from what?" I asked, naturally enough.

"From the life I've left behind me," he said.

And that is how I met Rush Rogers, who came in for an afternoon's call between booms, and stayed two years, until his death.

Rush was a strange person to be working in the woods. I know a slew of woodsmen, and most of them I like. But they are, by and large and with some exceptions, uneducated, superstitious, and lacking in what is generally called Culture, although they are almost invariably kind, courteous, and chivalrous. Rush was different.

He was the son of a multi-millionaire in the days when even one million dollars was a lot of money. (It still would be to me, if I could picture it. I like to keep my imagining down to practical sums, like the $47.95 Sears wants for the coat I crave.) He attended one of the choicest of Eastern prep schools, and one of the best of the small New England colleges. (The one I'll send Rufus to, if he can get in, despite his father's Harvard background.) This isn't just a fancy tale Rush was telling for his own advantage. I've met half a dozen of his classmates, subsequently, and they all corroborate every word he said. Anyway, Rush wasn't a liar. He wasn't even a shader of the truth.

I won't bore you with too long an account of his life before he came to stay with us. I'll just fill in a little, which seems too bad, in a way, because he had some fascinating tales to tell of the years when he devoted his life to tennis, the time he spent under Pershing chasing Francisco Villa over the sun-baked hills of Mexico,—where, as a private, he had an elegant and impractical silk pup-tent from Abercrombie and Fitch which he sold to a colonel at a handsome profit—and his career in the first World War, that little skirmish (remember?), from which he emerged a major. While in France, he met and married a Russian countess, a refugee. (I know this sounds like the worst and most lurid type of fiction, but can I help it if it's true?) He brought her back to this country.

She must have been a wonderful woman, because through her influence he became serious for the first time in his life. After the birth of his son, he decided that something was wrong with our educational system, and that since he had a boy of his own coming along now, he'd better do something about it. He had plenty of money, remember, and an excellent education; and, although he didn't yet know it, he was a born teacher. He opened a small private school, where he and a few masters undertook to teach little boys to be useful and intelligent citizens, as well as gentlemen and scholars. Most of the classes were held outdoors, which in the '20's was quite a departure. For English Composition, instead of the usual stupid "What I Did On My Vacation," the boys individually wrote letters to outstanding athletes of the day, asking such questions as "What is your definition of a good sport?" Rush showed me the answer they received from Lou Gehrig. I wish I had it to quote. It was a simple, thoughtful, wonderful letter, a good basis for half a dozen discussion periods on practical ethics.

Then one afternoon when Rush was waiting on the porch of the Country Club, after tennis, for Mrs. Rogers to pick him up, someone came and told him that both his wife and son had been instantly killed in a grade-crossing accident.

I once heard a woman of my acquaintance criticized severely for going to a dance a month after the death of her child. I resented that criticism. I happened to know that the woman was almost insane with grief. In my opinion, any method she chose to use as therapy was all right with me. If she wanted to dance, and it helped her at all, good. My attitude was that no one was in a position to criticize. All we can ever do is say how we *hope* we'll act under any given set of circumstances. We never *know* until the circumstances overtake us; and then we will, most likely, not act as we had hoped.

Rush's therapy was a resort to the bottle. His family had been all his life. He loved his wife, but he was simply crazy about his son. It must have seemed to him that everything important had been taken from him, and that nothing mattered any more. This was regrettable, but certainly not deserving of any moral judgment. In a few years he had wasted most of his fortune, and had also decided that while you can drink yourself to death, it isn't the best form of suicide, being both protracted and painful. That is why he came to work in the woods, at hard outdoor labor, far from the nearest saloon.

I'm not quite sure how his visit was protracted from an afternoon into two years. I remember he finished the log drive, and then, on Ralph's invitation, stayed for the week-end. They became involved in a wall-building project, which lasted more than a week. Then some friends were coming to visit us, one of them from Rush's old school, and Ralph thought the two men would enjoy each other. (They did. They had a wonderful time hashing over the olden days.) Then a concrete-pouring job came up, and after that there never seemed to be a convenient time for him to leave. We were always half-way through something important; and besides, Rush had somehow fallen into the habit of always helping me with the dishes, teaching Rufus the alphabet, and training the dogs to heel.

In case you want to know what he looked like, before we go further, he looked exactly like Lionel Barrymore, the spit'n'image, as we say here; so that he was frequently asked for autographs—which he furnished or not, depending on his mood at the moment. And as for what he was like, all I can say is that he was the nearest thing to a brother that I ever had. I could discuss things with him, over the dish-washing, that would have bored Ralph to profanity. Rush would give me his considered opinion on any number of trivial matters, such as whether I should dye the living-room curtains orange. Ralph, when asked, would say, "*I* don't care what you do. That's your department. Suit yourself." That's all very well, but sometimes I doubt my own taste, and it's nice to have another viewpoint expressed. We also sang hymns while we did the dishes. Ralph thought we were absolutely off our rockers, but it was rather fun to see who could remember the most verses of "A Mighty Fortress Is Our God" or "Rock of Ages." We'd both had church-going childhoods, and it was surprising how much came back.

One Christmas Rush and I decided to make fruit cake for the holiday. I found a recipe in a very old, beat-up cook-book, and we read it over. People did things on a grander scale in the last century, and at the end of the reading I said, "Gee, Rush, this is going to make an awful lot of cake. We'll never get rid of it."

"Oh, I don't know," he said. "My mother's cook used to make a cake that sounds like this. Then she put some of it down in crocks with rum, and that kept for months. The odds and ends she steamed and served with hard sauce, like plum pudding. She never threw any away."

"Okay, let's make it," I capitulated. "If it's no good, probably the dogs will eat it."

It took us two days to get the fruit prepared. We stoned raisins and chopped candied peel and citron until we were blue in the face. When it came to mixing the batter, I didn't have a bowl large enough, so we had to use my big aluminum boiled-dinner kettle. To bake it, we had to use every pan in the house, and that took a whole day, as my oven at that time wasn't any too spacious. In the end we had *acres* of fruit cake, and I thought happily of the months and months ahead when I wouldn't have to worry about the cake situation. Because the cake was good. Good, heck. It was perfect.

That was the trouble. It was gone within four days, gone with our plans for bottled-in-bond cake and steamed puddings to last until spring.

This sounds like a pretty simple tale, and it is. But unless you have been there yourself, you don't know how much difference there is between whipping up an easy little one-egg cake all alone, and making a great big fruit cake with someone who is interested in it, too. The first is a routine chore. The second is a social event in a country where social events are few and far between.

But there was one thing that I'd remember Rush for with affection and gratitude, even if he'd never lifted a finger in the kitchen, or taught Rufus to tell time and count to one hundred, or in general lent a hand indoors and out. It was the affair of Thor.

Thor was an enormous broken-to-harness Siberian husky that we'd been given to serve as teacher to the three huskies we already owned, with the idea of developing a sled-team, so we wouldn't have to pack all our groceries two miles on our backs in winter. At least, that was our idea when we accepted him. The idea of the donor was simply to get rid of the dog before becoming involved in a series of expensive damage suits. Thor was not vicious or dangerous. On the contrary, he was almost simple-minded, he was so good-natured and loving. But he was just too big and too full of boyish high-spirits to make a very successful pet in a suburb. He didn't make a very successful teacher, either. He was willing to do all the work, and the other dogs were more than willing to let him. So we gave up the dog-team idea and let the lazy oafs develop their talents as pets.

Then, just after we'd completely given our hearts to him, Thor made the grave mistake of trying, city slicker that he was, to swallow a porcupine whole. We'd had quill trouble before, but nothing like this. Usually, with a little patience, we'd been able to pull most of the quills out; and the few we didn't get would eventually suppurate and work out by themselves. This time it was hopeless. The dog's whole mouth and throat were solid with them. Even the services of a vet would have been useless, and we couldn't get Out to a vet at that time of year. There was only one thing to be done. The dog must be destroyed.

By this time Thor had crawled under a shed and refused to come out. We could see him there in the dark, his eyes wild and glazed with pain as he clawed at his mouth and groaned, but the space was too small for any of us to enter, and the angle made a sure, merciful shot impossible. I finally said, "You boys go away. We're all just making him nervous, standing here. I think maybe

I can get him out alone." I'd always fed the dogs, and in order to summon them to meals, I'd always whistled the only way I can whistle, through a space in my front teeth. It doesn't sound like much, being a sort of shrill hissing, but apparently it carries a long way, at least to a dog. So I went down to stand on my accustomed place, the kitchen steps, and hissed.

There was a scrambling under the shed, and Thor came out. He stood a moment, shaking his great head, and then he galloped across the clearing, his tail curled high, his whole bearing trustful and eager as he came up to me, who had always been his friend. Ralph caught him and took him away, and I heard the sound of one shot. That was all.

And then, with no warning, I began to cry harder than I have ever cried in my adult life, and I couldn't stop. Ralph and Rush, pretty sad themselves, came in and stood around looking helpless and embarrassed and offering me drinks of nice cold water and not too clean handkerchiefs, and all I could say was, "I'm sorry, don't mind me, I'll get over it. It's only that I—" And then I'd start howling again. I was ashamed of myself, but that didn't stop me.

"Look, Louise," Ralph said reasonably, "it was the only thing we could do. You know that. It was the merciful thing." I nodded speechlessly. I did know. "We've lost dogs before," he went on, "and you never acted like this." And that was perfectly true, too. "Now stop. You're going to make yourself sick." I couldn't make myself much sicker, I thought.

I tried to explain again. "I know, but this—He—I—" and choked on the words. I must have been a pretty sight.

Then Rush said quietly, "I know, Louise. You feel like

a Judas. You feel that he trusted you, and you betrayed him." And of course, that was exactly how I did feel, and why I was crying. If he hadn't come so eagerly and hopefully when I whistled to him, I could have stood it. Probably it was childish and silly of me, but I couldn't help it. "We'll get supper," Rush said. "Why don't you go take a walk?"

I took a long walk, half-way to B Pond, and when I got back, I felt better. I'll never forget Thor, and I'll never forget how understanding Rush was.

Three weeks later, Rush, too, was dead, killed in a hotel fire in Rumford. It was a terrible and shocking way for a so fundamentally kind and gentle person to die. It took us all a long time to get over it.

Rufus was too little to understand what had happened, but perhaps he missed Rush most of all. Rush was *his* friend first, the nice man he'd brought home to Mummy and Daddy, the man who helped him to make snowmen in winter, and formed shadow rabbits on the wall for him, holding up his hand with two fingers for ears in the golden light of the lamp; who played "This is the way the farmer rides" with him, bouncing the child on his outthrust foot until he shrieked with joy. Rush had been his special property, his very first private friend.

After Ralph died and Rufus was old enough to go to school, I had to make some sort of arrangement for his education. Catharine Gerrish was working for me then, so I rented a succession of furnished houses in various towns on the Outside, and installed her and her son, Vaughn, and Rufus (and soon Dinah) in them. I lived back-and-forth. In other words, I lived alone in the woods until I simply *had* to see the kids, when I'd descend on them for a visit. The last of the houses we lived in was at Rumford Point.

Rumford Point is a very small and very pretty village on the Androscoggin. There is one General Store and Post Office combined, which also serves as a social center. All the men who aren't working because of the weather, or a dropped stitch in the back, or whatever reason, congregate in Johnnie Martin's store to gossip, or maybe simply to sit in silent communion. Strange as it seems, Rufus, the son of solitude-loving parents, is extremely gregarious. Or maybe it isn't so strange. Maybe it's just the swing of the pendulum, along the line of the theory that ministers' sons often turn out to be hellions. At any rate, when Rufus was only in the second grade, he used to hang around the store a lot, chopping it up with the men. If you sent him over to buy a bar of soap, you could bet money that you'd have to call Johnnie up when your patience wore thin, and ask him please to send Rufus home. Most of the time Rufus said, when asked, that he'd been talking with Mr. Thomas.

Mr. Thomas, it turned out, was an elderly Negro. He was badly crippled with arthritis, so that he had to walk slowly and painfully, with the aid of two canes, over the snowy and icy roads of the Point. But that didn't seem to affect his disposition. He was a kindly, quiet-spoken man with a shy, pleasant smile, and the children liked him very much. His father had been a freed slave, brought back from the Civil War to this little New England hamlet by the local hero of the times, an officer in the Union Army. This sparse and forbidding country, with its stony fields and bleak prospects and frigid winters, must have seemed very strange to the boy from the lush South; but even more strange must have seemed to him the terms on which he was accepted. I have talked with men who knew Clarence Thomas' father, and they stated unanimously that he was a fine man. That's all. Not a fine man, considering. Just a fine man. You can't arrive at a judgment like that unless you have dealt with a person over a long period on terms of equality. The same judgment stands for his son, for the same reasons.

Mr. Thomas was the first colored person my children ever saw in their lives, and while I gave the fact no particular thought at the time, I now realize what a wonderful thing for them it was. No matter where they go, or what they read, or how much biased talk they hear, they won't be able to believe that there exists any race barrier that can't be overcome by understanding. After all, they knew that gentleman, Mr. Thomas.

And I, because I was their only parent and as such must take a double interest in my children's friends' suitability, knew him, too; and for me, too, it was a wonderful thing. As we grow older, the bright and passionate convictions of our eager youth tend to become overlaid with the rust of time and worn thin by the friction of dusty everyday living. Through the children's friendship with Mr. Thomas, my beliefs were restored to me in greater strength than ever.

CHAPTER FOUR

. . . *Four-footed As Well As Two"*

MY children are simply animal mad, and it's a lucky thing for me that I'm not allergic to any form of fur or feather, or I'd be sneezing all the time. It wouldn't do me any good to clamp down with a ban on pets. I'd just be asking for trouble, and I firmly believe that one way of maintaining discipline is to refrain from issuing any ukases that you can't enforce. If I didn't allow the children to have pets, they'd simply bootleg them.

Not so very long ago, I did say no to a request for white mice. I, too, am an animal-lover, but mice I can do without. A few nights later Rufus came in from the movies looking very smug and secretive, and retired immediately to his room. I went to investigate, and found him playing with an ordinary house mouse. It had been running around his feet at the movies, so he'd caught it in his hands and brought it home in his shirt pocket. Two or three days later, it—so to speak!—escaped, and has not been seen since. Then recently Dinah had a bad enough cold so that I put her to bed. She begged me to get her a turtle to play with during her incarceration, but that was in the winter, when no pet shops had turtles for sale. It seems they are a seasonal crop. She took my failure to provide with fair equanimity, which I put down to her being sicker than I had thought. In fact, this compliant attitude of hers contributed to my decision to call the doctor the next day. When she heard that Dr. Blumenthal was coming, she dived under her pillow and drew out a small pill box.

"Here," she said, "hide this somewhere. The doctor will raise the roof if he finds it. You know how he feels about taking pets to bed."

In the box, nibbling on a begonia leaf that Dinah had snitched from her grandmother's plant, was one of those fuzzy brown and black woolly bear caterpillars. She'd found it one mild day, wandering around in the sun, and had been keeping it *in camera,* in a manner of speaking, ever since. I connived at the crime, hiding it from the doctor and letting her play with it between times. I will admit, though, that I felt slightly queasy during Fuzzy's exercise periods, when she let him walk up one arm, across her shoulders, and down the other.

P. S. A few days after her recovery and return to school, Fuzzy also turned up inexplicably missing.

This just gives you a notion of what I would be up against if I said, "No pets." But I have no intention of saying any such thing. I like animals, too; and there is too little love and pity for the small and dependent and weak in the world to-day. If having the care and responsibility of a few animals is going to encourage these traits in my children, they can keep pigeons in the parlor, for all of me. I wasn't even too irritated when at the age of four Rufus woke me up in the middle of a rainy night to tell me that the robin who was nesting in the eaves of the ell at Forest Lodge, just outside his window, was getting wet and that he was going to lean out and hold an umbrella over her until it stopped raining. I explained that robins have feathers that shed water like raincoats; and besides, if he himself didn't get soaked and catch pneumonia, he'd probably fall out of the window and break his neck. It took about an hour to convince him. Maybe he never was convinced, because by that time it had stopped raining anyhow. He may sound goofy, but me, I prefer him to the boy who pulls wings off flies or torments cats.

I maintain that he is unique in the annals of modern times. I will bet that he is the only man, woman, or child alive to have been bitten in the ear at the age of six months by a skunk while, moreover, lying on the living-room floor of his parents' home.

You see, at that time we had a pet skunk named Rollo, whose mother had mislaid him along the Carry Road during a fight with one of the dogs at the hotel. Ralph brought him home in a paper bag, and since he was too young to eat out of a dish, we bottle-fed him for a while and turned him loose with a litter of Siberian husky pups we had at the time. Rollo was also too young to have developed the usual skunk method of protection, fortunately; and I think he believed that he too was a husky puppy, from the way he rough-housed and played and slept and ate with the dogs. I was always plunging into the melee to rescue him. Since he weighed about eight ounces, and the pups tipped the scales at ten pounds apiece, I feared for his life. He didn't thank me. The

Rufus woke me up in the middle of a rainy night to tell me that the robin who was nesting in the eaves of the ell just outside his window was getting wet and that he was going to lean out and hold an umbrella over her until it stopped raining.

minute I put him down at a safe distance, he'd shake himself and race back to the fray. I think he had a bad psychosis or trauma or whatever you call it, from having been left lost and alone during those terrifying hours before Ralph brought him home. He hated to be alone. If there was no better company at hand, he'd follow me around while I did my housework and badger anyone he saw sitting down with a book in hand to pick him up and hold him. He was a sweet, neat little pet, and we loved him.

It was as a result of this traumatic condition that Rufus got bitten. There was a thunderstorm that afternoon, so we were all in the living-room, waiting for it to stop. I had the baby lying on a blanket on the floor, and Rollo, his pals the pups being out in the woodshed with their mother, curled up beside Rufus' head for company. At an especially loud clap of thunder, Rufus rolled over and crowded Rollo, who, startled, bit his ear. He did no real damage, barely drawing blood, and Rufus never held it against him.

We were sorry to lose Rollo, but it was inevitable. As he grew older, toward the end of the summer, his true noctural skunk nature began to develop. He'd sleep days and roam around nights. Then he took to staying away from home for two or three days at a time. Finally it got so we saw him only once every week or ten days. Sometimes he'd come home for a chocolate malted milk, his favorite food, which he must have been daunted to learn did not grow on bushes or come bubbling out of the ground. Sometimes when we were walking along the Carry Road he'd hear and recognize our voices and come galloping out of the bushes to us. This certainly caused consternation and confusion among any of the summer people who happened to witness the reunion. There'd be a fine scurrying for climbable trees, and the air would be rent with shrieks, when we picked up our pet and cuddled him against our necks.

"One of these days," we'd be warned, "you're going to pick up the wrong skunk, and *then* you'll be sorry!" That was perfectly silly. How could you mistake the identity of one who had shared your bed and board for months?

Eventually winter came, Rollo went into the partial hibernation of skunks, and we never saw him again.

There is a school of thought that it is too much trouble to have pets. They are a care and a responsibility and a lot of bother. Well, so they are. So are children a care and a responsibility and a lot of bother, but we who have them seem to find them rewarding. I think that the keeping of pets is also worthwhile, but that is only one woman's opinion. Myself, since I have to stay home anyhow and take care of the kids or arrange for someone else to take care of them, I might just as well have a few animals to enjoy as well.

We've had a variety of pets, as the years have gone along. Once we had two Cochin China bantams sent us from California, and very handsome they were, too. They had been shelled by the Japs. Remember that time a Japanese submarine dropped a couple of shells in California, presumably doing no damage? Well, the shells landed near the coop of these bantams, damaging their *amour propre* considerably. The owner thought it imperative to find a new home for them, as far removed from the scene of shock as possible. He didn't know anybody in Maine, which he had picked as the ideal geographical

There is a school of thought that it is too much trouble to have pets. They are a care and a responsibility and a lot of bother. Well, so they are. So are children a care and a responsibility and a lot of bother, but we who have them seem to find them rewarding.

location for them, but he had read a book of mine, so he sent them to me. I don't think that a three thousand mile trip in a crate helped their nerves much, but they arrived in good physical condition, aside from a slight tendency toward hysteria for insufficient cause. However, by the middle of August they had settled down, and the little hen was laying her head off, bless her heart. Rufus had a bantam egg for breakfast every morning. Then a coon got the cock, the hen went into a decline from loneliness, and we gave her to a farmer, so she could have the company of his flock. She recovered her health and spirits, and the last I heard was doing well.

Then we had four rabbits, one black, one red, one gray, and one chinchilla. The mother of a little friend of Rufus' whom we had invited to visit him dreamed up the notion that they'd make a nice host present and sent them In with her son. I suspect she just wanted to get rid of the things. We liked them. At first we tried to keep them in a hutch and run, but they were always escaping. When this happened the entire household, including Ralph and me, the children, a hired man, a carpenter, and the cook, dropped everything to chase and catch them. Finally Ralph informed me that he wasn't paying carpenters' wages for having rabbits chased. Using a slide-rule, he'd figured out that every time the things escaped it cost us about $25, counting loss of time by the carpenter and assistant and cook, cessation of my productivity in the literary field, and waste due to burned cookies and other pastry. So we just let them loose. It didn't make any difference. They stayed in the clearing and slept in their hutch at night. But for several years after that, rabbit hunters and trappers were mystified by strange deviations from the normal wild snow-shoe rabbit indigenous to these parts. Our native rabbits are brown in summer and white in winter. What were being shot and trapped were almost any color you could mention, including plaid.

And cats. There is nothing unusual about a cat, and we have had so many that I can't begin to remember them all. There was only one that I really liked, a little coon-kitten that Alice Miller's father gave me. The coon-cat is peculiar to Maine, I believe, and people tell me that you can't very successfully move them to other places, although I don't know how true this is. I don't know why they are called coon-cats, either; I doubt if they have any raccoon blood in them. They are very handsome, with medium long hair, of a characteristic texture very rich and thick, and a solid, chunky build, unlike that of common cats. Usually they have tiger or tortoise markings. They are also unusually intelligent and make especially good mousers.

We named our kitten Mack, but shortly changed his name to Slapsy Maxie, because that was the way he acted. He was the only cat I have ever known who was a natural clown. Most cats esteem themselves too highly to make fools of themselves purposely, and unless you don't mind making a fool of yourself, you'll never be a top-flight comedian. This applies to people as well as to animals. Slapsy didn't give a hoot, as long as he got his laughs. He'd spin around on the top of his head in the middle of a room until he became dizzy, and then reel about with his eyes crossed, literally. If we laughed at him, he'd do it again, as soon as he got his breath and bearings. If we didn't laugh, he'd crawl under a chair and think up a new trick, like getting his head into a shoe and pretending not to be able to get it out again.

That was the summer when I was having so much trouble with my children. I don't know what it is about authorship, but the minute you've written a book people think you're something special. My two little darlings were the willing victims (by association) of this sort of thing and quite spoiled. I actually overheard them bragging to strangers that they were in a book.

One afternoon during this unfortunate period my sister and I were in the yard talking with some strangers who wanted to view the scene of a book of mine, "We Took To The Woods," when Slapsy went into his act. He jumped into an empty tub and commenced chasing his tail around and around inside it, like water in a centrifuge. Finally he peered over the edge with his eyes crossed, and then flopped over on his back and played dead. We laughed, so he got up and did it all over again.

My sister turned her back and lighted a cigarette. "Hmph!" she said with disapproval. "Now *he's* catching it. If that isn't an I'm-Mrs.-Rich's-little-cat routine, I never saw one."

I looked at the children and they looked at me. They were bright enough to get the point, and not too hardened in crime to feel abashed. After that, when I saw signs of their getting too big for their boots, I simply had to refer to Mrs. Rich's little show-off cat to bring them back into line. Maybe that's why I liked Slapsy so much. I could depend on him to serve as whipping boy. To any who may suspect from his behavior that he was subject to fits, I wish to state emphatically that he was *not!* The very idea!

He had his eye on the ball constantly and knew what he was doing every minute of the time.

But sometimes I have found myself in jams I hadn't planned on, because of our pets. After Kyak, the best dog we ever had, died, just before the Christmas we spent at Rumford Point, I decided that I would get each of the kids a pup for Christmas and call it a day. The kids in question were my own two and Vaughn, the son of Catherine, who was living with me at the time. I went to a kennel and bought two airedales for the boys and a springer for Dinah. The new acquisitions were a great success, and the next week was spent in a general making of friends.

Then New Year's Eve came up. Everybody, including Catherine, seemed to be going to a party that night, and the children wanted to go partying, too. I said I wasn't going anywhere, but that didn't seem to comfort them much. If I wanted to be a stick-in-the-mud, all right. That was my privilege. *They* wanted a party.

Finally I said in desperation, "Look, we'll have one to-morrow. It's too late to plan anything to-night. To-morrow we'll have any kind of party you want."

"Oh, boy! Can the dogs go?"

I said no, not unless they had it at home. If we had it at home, fat chance we'd have of keeping them away.

"What can we have to eat? What time will we have it?"

"Any time you want," I said foolishly. "And anything you want to eat that I can get."

The three of them retired to another room and made their plans, of which they apprised me shortly. They had decided to make it as early as possible: a breakfast party, in fact. And they had decided to have ice cream and gingerale; and they had decided to hold it in my bed, because it was nice and big. As soon as they awoke, they'd all come get into bed with me.

"Oh, *no!*" I moaned. "No! *Not* ice cream and gingerale in my bed at crack of dawn!"

Three pairs of eyes looked at me steadily and censuriously. "You *promised.*"

I had promised. I went and looked into the refrigerator to see what the ice cream and gingerale situation was against the coming debacle. There was plenty, I was sorry to see.

Well, a happy, happy New Year to you all; but if you take my advice you won't get roped into any breakfast-in-bed parties for the first morning of the bright new year. I can think of nothing less appetizing than vanilla ice cream and gingerale at six in the morning, and nothing less restful than three small children and three lively puppies to share your bed with you on that salubrious day. Wow!

That was one more occasion on which I could have used another parent for my children. If Ralph had been alive, he wouldn't have let me make any such fool promise in the first place. He had more foresight and a less impulsive mind and nature than I have. If, while his back was turned, I'd made it anyway, he'd have rallied 'round and taken some of the heat off me. Two people can usually stand and even enjoy what is a grueling ordeal when you're alone.

But now that the wound has healed, more or less, I'm glad I did it. The children had fun, even if I didn't. And a little while later Vaughn and Catherine moved away, and Rufus' airedale died of distemper, leaving nothing behind but a delightful memory—to them, at least—and Dinah's dog Patches.

That Patches! As I have said, he was an English springer, with the universal spaniel characteristics of sad, sad eyes and a fawning manner. He was very pretty, liver-colored and white, with long ears and a beautiful marcel; but he wasn't my favorite dog in the world. I like my dogs bigger, with more dignity. Patches was rather a fool. I took him visiting once, to some friends of mine who owned a canary, and he stood in the middle of the living-room and pointed the darn bird for hours, holding his point perfectly until he dropped from exhaustion. In the meantime the canary was having a nervous breakdown, so we had to banish Patches to the woodshed and put a dark cloth over the cage to calm the canary.

Then one spring I took him In to Forest Lodge with me to keep me company over the spring break-up of the ice on the lakes. He kept me company, all right. Every afternoon he'd sit and look at me with tears streaming down his face, begging me to take him for a walk. I'd say, "Go on for a walk yourself. I'm doing my spring house-cleaning." But he wouldn't, so I'd have to leave my windows half washed and tramp all over the lake region with him. I certainly got plenty of exercise that spring, and I had to give up fishing. Every time I made a cast, he'd jump joyfully into the river and retrieve my fly, scaring the living daylights out of every fish within ten miles. It was bad enough when he did that to me, but he took to following anyone he saw with a rod, after the ice went out and the spring crop of fishermen came In, and performing the same service for them. If you know any rabid fishermen, you realize that this would not be much appreciated.

Moreover, he would never learn about porcupines. Almost any other dog I ever had would learn after one experience that those things are burny-burny. Not Patches. He'd get involved daily, and I'd have to de-quill him, or if the case was really bad, take him Out to the vet. I once even had to go so far as to hire a Piper Cub to come In and fly that dope and me Out to Bethel. We both enjoyed the ride very much, but that's not the point. The point is that he just was no dog for this wild country, so I set about finding a new home for him. A friend of mine who was staying at the hotel was looking for a dog for his twelve-year-old son, so I said he could have Patches, if he'd promise to give him a good home.

"Well, it's like this, Louise," Curry said. "I don't care much for dogs myself, but George is an only child, and I think he ought to have one, don't you?"

I said that I did, and after a little talk with George, who promised on his Scout Honor to take full responsibility for the dog and not leave all the dirty work for his mother to do, and to treat him well, I turned him over. I said that when the Rogers returned to the hotel the following month, if I were not satisfied with the dog's appearance and bearing, I would snatch him back.

That dog must have had something not apparent to me. The next month the Rogers came back, and I had an interview with Patches. He was looking extremely well, not too fat and groomed within an inch of his life, and he was obviously fond of George and obedient to him. So I said it was a deal and turned over his papers and pedigree, making it official. Curry followed me out of the hotel office, where this transaction took place, to my old jallopy, parked by the iris bed.

"You know, Louise, that's a *wonderful* dog. He's almost human. He understands every word you say."

"I thought you didn't like dogs," I commented snidely.

"I don't. I don't like them at all. But Patches is exceptional. Why, the other morning—"

At the end of the story, which—if Curry will pardon my saying so—was exactly like all the stories dog-owners, myself included, tell to illustrate the superiority of their darlings, I made a rude noise and drove away home.

But of course that was unfair. Curry had never owned a dog before, so he didn't really know whether he liked dogs or not. Almost any dog is a good dog, if you want to put some time into his training, and if you pay attention to him and talk to him and love him. You get just as much out of dog ownership as you put into it; a principle which applies to almost any relationship in the world, with pets, with children, with people, with gardens, or with ideas.

Children don't come under the heading of pets, precisely, but much the same principles apply to them. Considering that we live mostly in Maine, I see nothing to be gained by sending mine to summer camp, as here we have better swimming, better woods, better everything than most summer camps do, except the companionship of contemporaries. To make up for this lack, I arrange for Rufus and Dinah to entertain friends of their own ages during the summer; and believe me, these visitations certainly revolutionize my own life. I have never had any particular ambition to become a camp counselor, but that is the role in which I find myself frequently. I wouldn't complain so bitterly if this role involved only such things as teaching basket weaving, the game of croquet, or how to make up a camp cot properly. But there really should be a man around the place to deal with the more robust and red-blooded aspects of life in the wilderness among the savage young.

Two or three summers ago we had visiting us Terry, Janith, Lorraine, and Paul. I was chief cook, housekeeper, and bottle-washer, because I had decided that now that the children were old enough to be of some practical use and not to need constant supervision, I could do the work easily myself. Our little guests had been briefed that they were supposed to make their own beds, keep their own rooms tidy, fill the wood-box daily, and help with the dishes; and all that worked out very well.

But I went out into the yard one morning and discovered the children throwing stones at a snake. We have quite a few around Forest Lodge, all harmless. They are just little grass or garter snakes, and very helpful in keeping down the insect and rodent population. I quickly donned my Nature Study Counselor face.

"You kids cut that out," I said, and went on to deliver a little homily on snakes are our friends and we should be kind to them. We certainly shouldn't throw rocks at them with murderous intent. They listened respectfully, and then Rainey wanted to know if I dared to pick one up, since they were so lovable.

Thought I: This is it, Rich. You asked for it, and it serves you right.

Said I, "Of course, dear. As I told you, snakes are our friends. There's no need at all to be afraid of them." The snake who had started this whole discussion had taken himself off, I was happy to note, so I need not be put immediately to the test. But I reckoned without my guests. They scattered, and it wasn't very long before I was summoned to the back of the clearing where they had discovered a garter snake sunning on a log. I don't need to tell you, do I, that I had never picked up a snake in my life; but I read both widely and indiscriminately, so I had a fair idea of the general procedure.

"Now this is the way you do it," I stalled along while I was getting up my courage. "You must be very careful to grasp the snake right behind where his ears would be, if he had ears. In that way, you prevent his turning his head to bite you. Not that it would be serious if he did," I added hastily, "since these snakes aren't poisonous. But it's just as well to do it properly." There didn't seem to be anything more to add, and the six intent young faces were displaying varying degrees of fascination and skepticism, so I took the bull by the horns—or rather, the snake by the ears.

My gosh, it worked! No one could have been more surprised than I. After an initial outraged thrashing, the reptile coiled himself around my arm and allowed me to stroke him into blissful quiet. I had always thought snakes would feel cold and slimy, but they don't. They feel dry and slightly cool, not unpleasant at all. After a few minutes I shook him off, he retired into the tall grass, I retired into the house, addressing myself complacently as Mrs. Ditmars, and the kids retired in six different directions to look for more snakes so that they could indulge in this intriguing sport themselves. The snake tribe sure took a beating that day.

Several hours later, as I was preparing dinner, they all

trooped into the kitchen, escorting Paul, who had made a hero of himself by getting bitten. He'd misjudged slightly and picked up a snake by the middle instead of the neck. Naturally his startled victim had turned around and nailed him, leaving a couple of very small marks.

"That's all right, Paul," I said. "It's nothing to worry about. These snakes aren't poisonous, as I told you. Just wash the wound thoroughly in soap and hot water and put on some iodine."

But Paul, who is a scholarly child, reads widely and his researches had given him a different view of the proper treatment of snake-bite. No, *not* a slug of whiskey. Informed opinion, he told me gravely, holds that that is the worst thing you can do to your patient, since alcohol stimulates circulation and spreads the poison throughout the system. You should cut open the wound and suck out the venom; and that was what he proposed to do. He picked up a large, very sharp butcher knife with which I had been cutting meat, and wiped it off with the dish cloth.

I put on my Camp Nurse manner. "Now wait, Paul. I told you there *is* no poison to suck out; but if you're bound and determined to go ahead, at least sterilize the knife first. Wash it in good hot soap and water and then sear it in the fire. That'll kill all the germs."

I guess he overdid it a little. The next thing I knew, he was hopping around with a nice burn on his wrist. I slapped on some soothing salve, and that was that. The next morning at breakfast, I inquired about his cut-burn-snake-bite, and he had a hard time deciding which hand had sustained the injury.

But picking up snakes is as nothing compared to some of the ordeals I, as Only Parent, find myself facing during these annual youth congresses. Take those rainy days when I find myself saddled with the role of Dance and Games Mistress. They are really brutal. In the first place, there is nothing I like less than card games; but I find myself not only organizing them, but also participating in them with what I hope is a convincing display of girlish enthusiasm. There is one particularly grueling game called Pounce which is a special favorite with the young, chiefly, I'm sure, because it calls for a great deal of screaming and pouncing. As many people can play as you have packs of cards, and unfortunately we have plenty. We sit around in a circle on the living-room floor before the open fire, each with a deck. Roughly, the plot is to get rid of your cards first, by playing them up from ace to king on piles in the center. You can see what happens when two people uncover a four-spot simultaneously and there is only one trey exposed. There are shrieks, a great slapping down of cards, and a howl of "Hey! I got mine down first. Look, Louise, look! Mine is under his. Make him take his back." I pronounce judgment, take another aspirin, and order the game to continue. Unless you have played Pounce with six children between the ages of eight and thirteen, you have no conception whatsoever of the meaning of the word bedlam.

As I said, I don't like to play card games, but I do. However, I simply *can't* sing, dance, or play the piano. I do, though. You ought to see and hear me. On second thought, no, I guess you ought not. It is very lucky that the young are so beautifully uncritical; or possibly they are simply tone deaf and lacking in aesthetic sense. On rainy days we have song-and-dance festivals sometimes when I can't get out of it. They are not noteworthy as demonstrations of grace and beauty, but they serve their purpose, which is to expend some of the bottled-up energy that a day of being cooped up in the house seems to generate.

The dancing takes place in the kitchen, because there is more room there and the floor is nice and solid, being laid over a concrete base. For music we either play the hand-cranking victrola or sing and clap our hands. We do folk dances, the more energetic and noisy the better: "Taffy Was a Welshman," "I Met My Love," "The Seven Steps," and everyone's favorite, even mine, "The Paw-paw Patch." The pans on the walls rattle, the rafters ring, and the windows shiver as we prance around bawling at the top of our lungs, "Where, oh, where is dear little Nellie?", coming in strong on the refrain, " 'Way down yonder in the paw-paw patch." I'll bet every deer in the county high-tails it for New Hampshire.

We have to do our piano playing and community singing in the kids' play-room. This is a room on the ground floor that used to be my winter living-room, and still is, when I'm here in winter. But when I acquired a piano, that seemed to be the only place to put it, and the room became automatically a game and play-room in summer.

Don't think for a minute that I went out and *bought* a piano. The possession of one wasn't that vital to my happiness. When I said acquired, I meant acquired. It was like this. Up in the office of the hotel there was a very ancient piano, for the use and entertainment of the guests, some of whom are excellent professional musicians. The old, tinny piano was a source of true pain to these. So a Piano Fund was conceived, and in the course of two or three years enough money was amassed so that a new, good piano could be purchased.

In the meantime Larry had been asking me on an average of about once a week how much I wanted for my old Essex, out of commission and resting on blocks in the lean-to that I dignify with the title garage.

"I don't know, Larry," I'd say. "I guess I'll hang onto it for a while. I might want to get it fixed up, in case the Ford folds."

"It'd cost more than the thing's worth, Louise, to put it on the road. It's a wreck. All I want it for is spare parts. That's all it's good for." He was right, but my Yankee nature made me loath to part with it, all the same.

Then one day I went up to the hotel and found Al cleaning out a room up-stairs with the idea of providing herself with more storage space. She was brooding over an old roll-topped desk, wondering what to do with it. It was the kind you used to see fifty years ago in the offices of country editors, varnished, ugly, capricious. I guess it was an eye-sore, but I immediately decided that it was exactly what I wanted. So I asked her what she'd take for it. She said I'd have to ask Larry.

I went and found him up in the light-plant house, tinkering on the Kohler, and put my question to him. He tested a bit of wiring thoughtfully. "Tell you what I'll do, Louise. I'll swap it for the Essex and throw in the old piano to boot. Your kids could have a lot of fun with that piano, and you don't want the Essex. I just want it for spare parts. I'll take the piano down to your house and tow the Essex back."

That sounded all right to me. I wanted the desk, I could

use the piano, and I'd managed to get along for several years without the Essex. In fact, I felt a little guilty about taking advantage of Larry, but he said that if I was satisfied, he was. So the next day the piano and desk were delivered, the Essex was hauled away, and I felt pretty smug about the whole thing.

I was a little dashed, two days later, to meet the Essex bowling merrily along the Carry Road under its own power. Spare parts indeed! I should have saved wear and tear on my conscience. Larry used it all the rest of that summer and part of the next. I didn't really mind, though. He did for himself, free, all the work on the jallopy that I would have had to pay for; and besides, I had and still have the desk and the piano.

It's quite a piano, at that. Of course it is completely out of tune, what with the damp springs and sub-zero winters. But it has a very special feature. By pressing down on a fourth pedal, you can accompany yourself on a banjo attachment. This is especially effective on such numbers as "Rock of Ages" or Handel's "Largo." We have a lot of fun with that beat-up old piano.

Picnics are all right taken in reasonable doses, but frankly I am not crazy about going on a picnic every single sunny day. That is what it amounted to, when my children were entertaining, until I made some new ground rules. The first was that I, personally, would picnic once a week, and on that occasion we'd take the car and go to Smooth Ledge, build a fire, and have a cook-out. The second was that the children were free to picnic or not, as they saw fit, on any or all of the other six days. I would put up cold lunches for them, which they could eat at any one of the Approved Picnic Spots—approved by me, acting now as Head Counselor or Great White Mother. This gave them plenty of leeway, since the Approved Spots ranged from the front porch, overlooking the river, downstream to Long Pool, and up-road to the cove in Pond-in-the-River where the lumber company had its tow-boat, the *Alligator,* pulled out. The third rule was that I would snatch them bald-headed—since I was in no position to say, "Wait till I tell your father"—if I heard of their being outside the limits of this Louise-defined reservation. They were my self-induced head-ache, and I didn't propose to have them annoying innocent bystanders, like my neighbors or the guests from the hotel.

This panned out very well, and the children ate an average of four lunches a week outdoors, leaving me to a peaceful and leisurely meal by myself. Then along toward the end of the summer they came to me in a body and said they'd like to take their lunches over onto the island across from the lodge. In order to get there, you have to walk up to Pondy Dam, cross the river on it, and back-track down the further bank until you come to the one place where the narrow back channel can be leaped. So it makes a fairly worthwhile expedition, and I had nothing against the plan, except that it looked to me as though it was going to rain. I suggested that they wait another day.

"Aw, gee, Ma. Gee, we have to all go back to school next week. We ain't got much time left. Gee, come on, let us go."

"Haven't much time," I corrected automatically. "All right, I'll put up your lunches, and if it starts raining, you can come home and eat them on the porch."

It started raining hard about half an hour after they set out, and I kept expecting them to return. When they didn't, I went out and took a look at the other side of the river to see what had become of them. I found out, all right. The whole six of them and Terry's dog, Chipper, were sitting in a row on a smooth ledge that was about a foot under water, eating. The river was boiling around their waists and chests, the rain was pelting down on their heads and shoulders, and they were stuffing down what must have been practically liquid sandwiches. I whistled and called, but they couldn't—or wouldn't—hear me over the noise of the rapids, so I shook my head and went into the house and the nice warm fire.

Two hours later they showed up, the most bedraggled crew I have ever laid eyes on. The minute they got into the house, they started telling me about the picnic, all talking at once. I finally made out that Rufus had skinned his knee, Janith had got stung by a hornet, Rainey eaten so much she had a stomach ache, Terry lost his tee-shirt in the river, Dinah swallowed an ant, and Chipper almost had cramps.

"Now, wait," I said. "Explain to me how you can tell when a dog *almost* has cramps. And while we're at it, explain to me why you were all sitting up to your gizzards in the river. I saw you, so don't deny it."

Paul looked at me with a twinkle in his dark eyes. "When it started to rain, we thought we'd better get under water to keep dry."

I drew a deep breath and then decided to skip it. "Well," I said instead, "I'm very sorry that your picnic turned out so badly, and that you didn't have a good time. Maybe to-morrow—"

Six dumbfounded faces turned to me. Dinah found her voice first. "Why, Ma, we had a wonderful time, the best time we've had all summer!"

Now I ask you. What can you do about children—except love and enjoy them?

CHAPTER FIVE

Return of the Native

IN order to explain why I have lived in Bridgewater, Massachusetts, during a large part of the winter for the past few years, I shall have to go into dissertations on (a) education and (b) grandmothers. It's not going to be very fascinating, so I'll be as brief as possible.

First, then, education. During the early years of their school lives, my children attended various rural schools hereabouts in Maine, because Forest Lodge was home, and I wanted them within hollering distance, so to speak. I know perfectly well that rural one- or two-room schools have educated some of the great men of our history; and I know also that in theory, at least, it isn't the school that matters so much as the quality of the teaching. During my kids' careers in rural schools, they were exposed to some very excellent and imaginative teachers, to whom I am grateful.

But these poor women were hampered by lack of equipment and facilities. The towns in which they taught were too poor to buy the best and newest educational aids, or else the school committees considered such things to be new-fangled and frivolous money-wasters, which their fathers would have given short shrift. What was good enough for father is good enough, period, is a philosophy that has a fairly tenacious grip on much of our local thinking; and for children who will grow up to be farmers or farmers' wives, possibly it is valid. I won't argue that, although I have noticed that those who yell this good-enough-for-father slogan the loudest, very often house in their barns, rather than the descendants of father's horses, the biggest and best tractors available.

Be that as it may, it is possible that my children may wish to explore wider fields than these, and I did not feel that the education they were getting was equipping them to do so. The teachers were good and they tried hard, but the day when a university consisted of Mark Hopkins on one end of a log and an eager student on the other are over. I will bet that I can change a tire better and faster than the best mechanic in the Western Hemisphere, *if* I have the proper tools and he is allowed only a hairpin and a tack hammer. By the same token, the best teacher needs more nowadays than her God-given talent, a paper, a pencil, and McGuffey's Reader.

Besides all that, most of the really good teachers don't stay long in these backwoods. They just cut their teeth here. As soon as they have a backlog of experience, they are hired away to communities which can afford to pay them decent salaries. I know this sounds treasonable to the country that I have loved and called home for almost twenty years; but the fact remains that what is good enough for me, an adult with background for comparison and a free choice of values derived from experience, is

I chose Bridgewater out of all the places available for the simple and obvious reason that it is my home town and my parents lived there. It's a nice town and there are a lot of very nice people indeed in it.

not quite good enough for my children. I spend hours practicing the subtle Maine way of pronouncing boat—which is somewhere between *bote, but,* and *boot,* and when I'm trying to be funny, I sometimes say *'twun't* for "It won't." I talk about keepin' a snug watch on the weather, when I mean that I am observing the sky, the winds, and the barometer closely for signs of precipitation; and I announce that I'm goin' to shove off 'fore it's dark under the table, when I mean that I intend to retire early to bed. This all amuses me mildly; but I have found myself to be less enchanted with local speech ways when my children employ them for want of any other. I like the way people talk around here, finding in it both economy and color. But if my children are going—as perhaps they will and perhaps they won't—to inhabit a larger, cosmopolitan world, it would be a good and helpful thing if they could speak the language with some fluency, purity, and grace. That is why, after Ralph died and I was making the decisions, I decided to continue their schooling in Bridgewater.

I chose Bridgewater out of all the places available for the simple and obvious reason that it is my home town and my parents lived there. And that brings us to grandmothers. After my father died, my mother was left alone. While she is a truly remarkable woman for her age, she is not a young woman—not young enough to cope easily with young children. Even if my kids were angels, which they are not, still I would not feel that I could saddle my mother with their sole care and discipline. She brought up her own family; why should she have to bring up mine? So for the past few winters I have hung around Bridgewater ready to crack the whip, administer the dose of milk of magnesia, or have a word with the Principal of the school, as occasion demanded.

The fact that Bridgewater does not exactly constitute my idea of heaven on earth is not the fault of the town, but rather of me. It's a nice town, about thirty miles south of Boston, and there are a lot of very nice people indeed in it. Some I have known from the cradle, and some I have met only since I have returned. They're not to blame because I'm not crazy about living in Bridgewater.

No, it's me, all right; or perhaps it's the life I have lived for the past seventeen years. It's very hard, when you have lived for almost two decades with no neighbor nearer than two miles, to remember to pull down the shades when you undress for bed, and that there is a prejudice in favor of being sufficiently clad for decency's sake when you wish to step out and take a look at the weather. It's also hard to impress upon your young, who all their lives have drunk out of the first brook they came across when they were thirsty, that no, dear, here we can't do that; you'll have to wait till you get home. I don't care if the water does look clear as glass, dear; germs are tiny things you can't see, but they can make you very ill—maybe even kill you. Now you heard me. I don't want any more argument! Things like that wear you down.

For years while I lived in the woods I owned one suit and one dress, which I wore on the rare occasions when I went Outside into civilization. The rest of the time I wore either dungarees or ski pants during all my waking hours. This costume is not considered high in style in Bridgewater, or in any other town, for that matter. So I have to get horsed up in a skirt and stockings if I intend to appear in the center of the town after noon. Mornings

I do affront the public with dungarees, if I have any errands to do in the village, and I seize upon a stormy day as a good excuse not to change my clothes after lunch. I know I am eyed askance, and it makes me slightly unhappy, but not enough so that I will mend my ways. Actually I sympathize with the beholder. I am not being judged on moral grounds, but on aesthetic. No woman of my size and age, wearing pants, is a vision of delight, I am well aware. So in Bridgewater I am constantly torn between comfort and appearance, the two being completely incompatible, in my case.

Costuming bothers me some, but not as much as the pressure. Alys Parsons and I once agreed that we were both spoiled for community living, and I now realize how right we were in thinking so. Where we come from, you do things when you want to do them. Since I write in the morning, I'm accustomed to doing my housework whenever it's convenient. I long ago abandoned and forgot the standard which judges a woman as being definitely slovenly, if not worse, if she doesn't have her washing on the line and her tubs emptied by ten o'clock on Monday morning at the very latest. If it's convenient for me, I start my laundry at four o'clock on Wednesday afternoon and leave it out all night to dry; or I wash floors at nine in the evening. Who cares? Nobody's going to drop in and discover me at my horrible practices. But among civilized people there is a time and place for everything, and life is simpler for you if you try to conform.

Then consider the matter of the telephone. When I lived alone in the woods, the thing we call a telephone rang infrequently. When it did, I knew it was either one of the Parsonses, Joe Mooney, or the Millers, since they are the only people on the line, and I knew that they wouldn't be calling me up unless they had something to say to me. Our average telephone conversation lasted two minutes at the most. Moreover, if the telephone rang while I was busy, I just let it ring, confident that if anything very vital was at issue, whoever it was would call me again later.

It's very, very different in Bridgewater. The telephone rings all the time. People call you up just to visit about nothing, or to try to dragoon you into participating in some project in which you have little if any interest, or to sell you something you don't want. It's no good to ignore the thing. Someone will answer it, and run screaming for you. I did once try to institute a system whereby my mother or the children would say, if the call was for me and I was writing, "She's busy working right now, but I'll have her call you later." This worked part of the time, but part of the time it resulted in great coolness toward me on the part of the caller. I'd be met with reproachful glances and restrained courtesy the next time we encountered. "Working, humph!" would be the thought behind this front. "She calls that working! Merely sitting in front of a typewriter! She could have taken a minute to answer the 'phone!"

I spend hours on the telephone in Bridgewater, and to date have transacted by this means very little business of any importance whatsoever. In its place the telephone is a very handy gadget, and there are circumstances under which it can be literally a life-saver. But the thing has got out of control. It's an incubus. Or maybe I'm just woods-queer and unconditioned for modern life.

I'm used to taking time in large chunks. You can do

that in the woods. You think to yourself, "To-day I'll finish chapter four,"—or paint the boat, or clean the shop, or whatever—and you go ahead and do it. Sure, it took six hours to scrape and paint the boat; but heck, you had six uninterrupted hours, whenever you wanted them. In civilization, you never have six free hours at a stretch. Time is doled out in smitches and dabs. You can snatch two hours here, before it's time to drive the kids to dancing school; or you can squeeze in an hour there, between lunch and the Heart Fund Tea you promised to attend. You live with an eye on the clock, and that isn't good. Clocks, like telephones, should be servants, not masters.

My idea of the really good life is the life I've been living for almost twenty years. It's a life dictated by nature. You get up when it's light, be it 5 or 8 a.m., and you go to bed when you're tired enough to sleep. You eat when you are hungry. You start a job and keep at it until it is done, allowing only weariness or hunger or unsuitable weather or a running out of the daylight to interrupt you. You take your fun where you find it, fishing or swimming or admiring the autumn foliage or swapping gossip with the game warden.—All right, all right, that's not Life; that's only existence. Nevertheless it is, to me, the comfortable and sensible way to live. A murrain on having to bathe and change your clothes at exactly 1:30 p.m. so that you won't be late to whatever-it-is, no matter what job has to be abandoned or what sentence left dangling like a windsleeve on a calm day.

This sounds very ungrateful and anti-social, and I guess it is. I'll just have to repeat that I'm ruined and peculiar. I'm just no longer geared for the life that is considered normal by most people, and my children never have been.

We've been seduced by mountains and space and snow and freedom. But since there's no way of telling where their lives will be lived, they might as well learn to adjust now, while they're young and still malleable. If they can learn to recognize the law of the pack at least well enough to give it convincing lip-service, they may be able to dodge a few knocks.

Bridgewater, as I have said, is a nice town; but more trouble can overtake us there, I swear, in any given stretch of time than anywhere else we've ever been. It must be a jinx. Take for example the events of one week during last September. On Monday, Dinah's cat, the darling of her heart and the pride of her life, died suddenly of what I diagnosed as poison. Dinah cried so terribly that she made herself ill. To comfort her, I told her she could have one of the Haskell's new kittens, and she went and got it immediately. Tuesday she woke up with a bad case of poison ivy and had to stay out of school. On Wednesday Rufus, riding his bike around a blind, hedge-shielded corner, was hit by a truck. He escaped with a few minor contusions and torn pants, but his bicycle was smashed to smithereens and the truck driver was reduced to a quivering jelly. He and I, both. On Thursday I broke my glasses, on which I am idiotically dependent. On Friday the new kitten died, and I decided against poison in favor of distemper, which it was; so we couldn't have any more cats until the joint was free of the virus, probably for a year. There was a great wailing at the wall by Dinah. Saturday Rufus went fishing with a couple of his cronies on a lake a little way out of town and lost overboard in the deepest part the new outboard I had bought for him only ten days before.

That tied up the week neatly, just in time to forestall my cutting my own throat. If there had been just one more day—! And in case you doubt this account, I can produce signed affidavit that it is absolutely true. I'll grant you that this sample week is hand-picked, but it is not immeasurably worse than a large proportion of those we have spent in Bridgewater. An acquaintance called me up one day in February and asked, just to be polite, how things were at our house. "At the moment, fine," I told her.

"No!" she exclaimed. "You mean no leprosy or chimney fires?"

That's the kind of a reputation we have in Bridgewater. The doctor worries about us if he doesn't have a call every three weeks or so. He starts inquiring around. It isn't that he suspects us of seeking the services of another practitioner, and he doesn't for a minute believe that we're all well. No, indeedy. He just begins to wonder if, unknown to the neighbors, we've all quietly succumbed to bubonic plague or been asphyxiated in our sleep. My children are the pictures of health, but that's a snare and a delusion if ever I saw one. Brought up in the germless paradise of the backwoods, they never had a sick day until they encountered civilization, and so had acquired no immunities whatsoever. They are pushovers for the puniest runt in any culture of germs, a fact well-known to the germ tribe and exploited accordingly. Any little toddler of a germ can come home at eventide and say to his big brothers and sisters, "Boy, what I did to-day! You know that big hulk of a Rufus Rich? Well, did I ever knock him for a loop!"

All this sounds pretty grim, but it's not as grim as it

sounds. Besides learning about civilized speech, manners, and deportment—which is really what they're here for—the children have a wonderful time. They're terrifically busy little bodies. In Maine they almost never had other children to play with. In Bridgewater there are droves of their peers all over the place. They belong to the Brownies and the Boy Scouts, and seem to be involved continually in cookie sales, paper drives, and all-day hikes. They attend dancing school and Sunday school and picnics and parties and football games. Then there are fire engines to chase, and stores to browse through, and occasional movies. I know all this seems very ordinary and tame, judged by usual standards; but my children's standards are not usual. They were brought up in a howling wilderness, and the largest town they ever lived in before had two general stores, a post-office, and a police force consisting of one constable, who didn't own a uniform, worked full-time on another job, and made perhaps two arrests a year. So you can see that the common material of average children's lives is the stuff of dreams-come-true to mine. Sometimes I think my poor kids are handicapped by their early lives; but more often I wonder if it wouldn't be a good thing for all children to live in seclusion for the first six or seven years. The glitter on the world lasts longer if they do.

And as for me—well, in almost any place imaginable, provided you are not under physical restraint and have your wits and health about you, you can find something to interest and entertain you. Bridgewater is no exception, although I will admit that I sometimes find myself standing off at a little distance from myself and wondering if this can possibly be I. This most frequently happens at PTA board meetings.

The reason that I am on the board of the PTA is because I was asked to be. While such an honor was furthest from my heart's desire, I thought I'd better accept. Otherwise I would in future be disqualified from opening my big mouth in complaint if some aspect of the local system of education met with my disapproval. Not that I anticipated such an occasion, but still and all, you never know. So once a month, at dinner time, I begin to groan about having to go to board meeting, and how did I ever get into this in the first place.

The peculiar thing is that when I finally get there, I have a good time. The other members are people I would not and do not ordinarily see. We're from different neighborhoods, of different religions, employed in different occupations, and, you would say, have nothing much in common. But starting out with a common interest in the welfare of our various children, we find a great variety of mutual interests. I've made several good friends by being on the PTA board.

Never having been a member of any board whatsoever before in my life, I have no idea how other boards behave themselves. I'd always had a picture of a long table surrounded by solemn faces and pompous manners, where business was conducted according to strictest parliamentary procedure, and where, after the motion to adjourn, —and how in the world did I ever get this idea?—a little man with a black bag went discreetly around distributing $20 gold pieces. The members, pocketing them absentmindedly, donned their silk hats and astrakhan-collared coats, bade each other formal adieux, and went on to their next board meetings. I must have read something in my youth to have given me this very vivid impression. "The Wolf of Wall Street," perhaps?

Our board meetings aren't like that at all. We attend clad in whatever we happened to have on—business suits, house dresses, golf slacks and windbreakers, silk prints, or dungarees. (Me.) We sit on desks and swing our feet, since most of us are too big for the seats in the class-room assigned for our use. We talk about the fall styles and the tomato blight and how-do-you-like-your-new-car and the bass fishing along the Cape Cod Canal. Nobody ever asks for the floor. If you feel like expressing an opinion, such as, "No, that's a bum idea," or, "Yes, that ought to work," you express it. At the end of the discussion, which is always animated but always free from animosity, someone says, "Sure, let's do that, then," and everyone nods. Then *almost* always the president remembers his duties and says diffidently, "Maybe we should put it in the form of a motion. Somebody, please?" After that someone else says, "Gee whiz! I've got to go home! I told my husband—" This counts as a motion of adjournment, and the meeting is ended.

Strangely enough, we accomplish something.

One of the projects we had in hand was to raise some money to help buy uniforms for the Junior-Senior High School Band. The kids and their instructor had worked hard and had a pretty good organization, and they deserved to look as well as they sounded. The chairman of the Ways and Means Committee, a capable and charming young woman, suggested a food sale, because, said she, you always made money on a food sale, an opinion which turned out subsequently to be correct. It would involve a lot of work, she added, and since her committee was small, we'd all have to help her. We all said we would, and the detail I drew was to drive around town on the morning of the sale, picking up the food that was being baked and donated by the members of the association.

I had a wonderful time. My first call was at the home of a lady with an unpronounceable Italian name, who was down on my list for two dozen cup-cakes. She had them ready, but she was just drinking her second cup of coffee—her first having been at 5:30 when she had to get Him off to work—and would I like one? I would, so we had a fine chat over coffee and hot, crusty bread, just out of the oven. She gave me an altogether fresh explanation of why my African violets wouldn't bloom. (Hers were beautiful.) All this watering from the bottom with warm water, all this moving them into and out of sunlight, all this fussing around, was so much unnecessary foolishness. I'd have to get rid of Dinah's cat. African violets refuse to bloom in the same house with a cat.

Well, take it or leave it. I never put it to the test. Get rid of Dinah's cat? Hah! (This was before the distemper.) Only the Grim Reaper managed to do that without severe repercussions to self.

My last call, though, was the one that really set me back on my heels. I was supposed to pick up an angel cake, way over on the other side of town. If I could make an angel cake, which I can't, you wouldn't catch me giving it— But that's beside the point. I walked up the steps of the address given and rapped on the door. My knock was not answered, a fact that didn't surprise me much, since the air for half a mile around was quivering with the sort of howls and shrieks that the very young can give off if sufficiently annoyed or frustrated. "Hmm. Temper," I thought, and gave the door a good belt. "If that were *my* child—" It's always very easy to think, "Hmm, if that were *my* child!", I've found.

The door swung open violently, to reveal a young and harassed man, with one screaming child under his arm and another apparently trying to bite his leg off at the knee. "Shut up!" he said. "What do *you* want?"

I chose to believe that only the last part of that was meant for me, and began rather hesitantly, "I'm collecting the donations for the PTA food sale, and Mrs. X promised an angel cake, so—"

He laughed a little hysterically. "You're out of luck, Sister. She ran away with the boarder yesterday, and I've got enough troubles— Shut *up,* will you?— I can't find no one to take care of the kids, so I'm home from work, losing pay, and the dishes ain't been done, and— Even if I'd known you were coming, I wouldn't have baked a cake."

Oh my, yes. PTA participation certainly opens amazing vistas.

Being a parent opens vistas in all directions, as far as that goes. And the Only Parent has special ones. When I hear the kid next door bragging, "My father can—" I feel sore at heart for my own children, who have no father to brag about. But I feel pretty good when I hear one of them say, "My mother says so," or, "My mother will—" That's how I discovered Titicut Village. Dinah told her teacher, Mrs. Higgins, "My mother will—", with a complete confidence that I would back her up. Well, whatever it was all about, of course her mother would!

In this case, I was well rewarded for volunteering to act as a teacher's helper.

It seems that the Fourth Grade had been studying Indians, and Mrs. Higgins, an excellent and competent teacher, was following up her class-room and background work with a field trip to Titicut Village, the site of an old Indian encampment, now being excavated by members of the Massachusetts Archeological Society. It's about two miles out of town, and when I was a kid we used to go there on our bikes, on picnics. To us it was just a ragged field and a pine grove on a bend of the Taunton River, a pleasant, quiet place. It had no name in those days.

It isn't a quiet place any more. Oh, I don't mean that the diggers are noisy and boisterous. On the contrary, they are very tranquil, busy people, sitting in their little pits, patiently scraping the earth away and sifting it for artifacts. No, the activity which fills the place is that of about three centuries ago, recreated vividly from the findings through the knowledge and imagination of the archeologists.

A Professor Robbins, a man afire with enthusiasm for his work if ever I saw one, showed us around, pausing first in the pine grove, where signs of recent digging were apparent. "This was the burial ground," he explained, and marked the thin, needle-strewn earth with the toe of his moccasin. "Right here we uncovered the skeleton of a boy of about sixteen, and the bones of his dog, buried with him." Somehow it was very real to us, as we stood there looking down, and the children started asking questions. Why was the dog buried with the boy? What kind of a dog? Were they killed together? Maybe they got into a bear fight. Or maybe—there are some brilliant imaginations in the Fourth Grade—the dog was drowning and the boy tried to save him. Aw, don't be a dope. Dogs don't drown, do they, Mrs. Higgins? More likely the boy was drowning and the dog tried to save him. Or maybe the dog died of a broken heart when his master died. My cousin's dog won't eat when he's away. Or maybe, I thought to myself, the boy so loved his dog that his parents, heart-broken at the contemplation of the long, dark and lonely journey ahead of their son's spirit, sent his dog along with him, to keep him company. But probably I was sentimentalizing.

"And here," Professor Robbins moved a little further into the grove, "was an interesting grave. The bones were in a remarkably good state of preservation. There's good drainage here, and light, dry soil. It was the skeleton of a young woman with gold coins in her ears. Of course the Indians hereabouts didn't have gold, so we know that she must have got them from a white trader. We don't know why, but we can make guesses." That man certainly knew how to arouse interest in the young, and in me, too. The guesses were on the lurid side. Maybe she saved a white man's life when he was lost in a blizzard. Maybe she killed and robbed him. Professor Robbins, strolling along in the rear of the little party with me, had another theory, not particularly suitable for Fourth Grade ears.

"Maybe she wasn't any better than she should have been, as the saying goes." He sighed. "But she had beautiful bones." He shook his head, thinking of that errant, copper-colored girl. "Probably she just got what she was asking for, a good throttling."

Now can't you just see that little hussy setting the village by the ears with her carryings-on? She must have had something, at that, to make a man regretful centuries after her death.

"Here was the work-shop," he told the class. "This was the place where they made their arrows and skin-scrapers. You can see all the chips lying around." He sifted earth through his hands, and showed us the quartz flinders, still sharp-edged and clean. "You children may pick up any of these that you want, to take home." And the class scattered like a flock of chickens picking up grain. "Arrow-heads weren't hard to make," he went on. "You could make them yourselves." He squatted, Indian fashion, on his heels. "You hold a large piece of quartz like this, and you take a smaller piece, like this, and you just press chips away—" Immediately we had a circle of intent little novices, busy making their first arrow-heads. They did pretty well, too; and I wondered if long ago a man with a brown skin squatted just there, surrounded by just such a circle, giving the same lesson. "Of course it takes practice," Professor Robbins said, rising and dusting his hands. "But you children could do it very easily."

Now we came out into the field where the active digging was. The diggers were scraping away tissue-thin layers of earth, each in his staked-off plot, and inspecting them for treasures. I have never seen a more absorbed and contented-appearing group of people. An extremely distinguished looking gentleman wearing one of the few Van Dyke beards I have ever met looked up as we approached.

"See what I've just found," he said with quiet satisfaction, and all the children gathered around, their faces alive with interest. It was an arrow-head of rose quartz, beautifully made, jewel-like in its color and perfection. I coveted it immediately—no, *not* to have set into a pin; just to hold in my hand and love. "Now how do you suppose that got lost?" the gentleman asked, looking up at the ring of faces around him. "Right in the middle of the camp, too. Someone was pretty upset about it, I'll bet."

That's what I like about archeologists. They can put themselves so fully into the past, into another person's shoes, even if those shoes were dust hundreds of years ago. Maybe that is the true definition of imagination: the ability to put yourself in another's place.

But what charmed me most about this gentleman was the fact that while he held in his hand the lovely bit of stone, he was listening to the World Series on a battery set at his elbow. And what's more, he was just as excited about the doings of the Dodgers as he was about his recent discovery. That's certainly living in two worlds.

One of the children asked, "Why aren't people digging over there?" And sure enough, in the middle of the field was a roped-off space conspicuously untouched.

"The accepted archeological practice," Professor Robbins explained, "is to leave some part of any digging for the future." He remembered the ages of his audience. "That is, we leave something for the next fellow. A hundred years from now, someone else may want to dig here. We leave something for him to find."

"Why?" asked a little realist. "Whillikers, maybe the best things of all are right where you're not digging."

"Maybe they are," Professor Robbins agreed gently. "But a hundred years from now, people are going to know more than we do. They're going to have better methods. Just recently rays were discovered by which the exact age of wood and bones can be determined. Before we had to guess, and some of our guesses were pretty bad. There'll be other discoveries, other methods developed—"

The little realist commented, "But that ain't going to do us any good."

"Not us, perhaps. But by leaving part of this ground alone, we're going to contribute to the eventual sum of human knowledge. In other words, boys and girls of your age, a hundred years from now, will know more than you do, if we just don't dig over there. Don't you think that's worth while? To help other children? Why, some of them may be your own grandchildren."

The class giggled delightedly at the ridiculous idea of any one of them ever having a grandchild, but they were impressed, nevertheless. So was I. While working and planning for Utopia was not a new idea to me, I had never had it brought home to me so simply and graphically. Standing here in this sunny autumn field, I felt for the first time that maybe we were on the way to a better world. If Professor Robbins' words stuck in the minds of even two or three of the children listening and even minutely influenced their adult conduct— But maybe I was just under the influence of the place and the hour.

I get involved in other things not so enjoyable through parenthood, like the ownership of a TV set, when I swore I'd never have one under my roof. I had to get it, for the protection of the neighbors. My neighbors are always nice to my children, but I doubt if they care to have the little Riches haunting their living-rooms every evening and most rainy afternoons. Then, since there are no movies in Bridgewater, I have to take my offspring to Brockton once in a while to a show of *their* choice, naturally. The things they choose. I've seen more darn cowboys and shooting affrays and cattle stampedes than you could shake a stick at. Two sticks. The only break I ever almost got was when they asked me if I'd take them to see a Gene Autrey movie. I said yes, I supposed so. When we got there, I discovered that the companion picture—and this seems an odd coupling—was "A Streetcar Named Desire," which I'd been wanting to see myself. My joy was very short-lived. It didn't take very many feet of film to convince me that this was not suitable entertainment for a girl of nine and a boy of fourteen. So we left.

Then there are the pets that die and cause universal mourning; and the birthday parties where you have to wear a paper cap and organize games of Hunt the Thimble; and the cereal you don't care for but have to eat for the sake of the box-top; and— But why go on? I'm managing to depress myself, and anyhow, every parent could recite the list in her sleep.

And like every parent, no matter how devoted she may be, I do have some life of my own. There are quite a few things in Bridgewater that I can do, independent of my children.

CHAPTER SIX

Time Out

IT was over a quarter of a century ago that I left Bridgewater to take a teaching job in New Hampshire, and until the problem of my own children's education reared its ugly head I had never been back except for brief visits. It was therefore out of the question for me to pick up where I had left off, when I came back here to live almost ten months of the year. Most of the boon companions of my salad days had moved away or married or both. In any event, we had grown apart, absorbed in our various and divergent ways of life, and had little in common except the past; and while the past is good for an amusing afternoon of "Do you remember the time—?" and "Whatever did become of her?", that is about all that it, *per se,* is good for. Just because thirty years ago Jane Jones and I shared a passionate interest in winning a silver cup for the Girl Scouts' Semaphore Team, spending hours a day wig-wagging "The quick brown fox jumps over the lazy dog"—a statement of no moment except that it employs every letter in the alphabet—back and forth to each other, we are not necessarily soul-mates to-day. She's a woman executive, shrewd, stylish, and dynamic, and I'm—well, what I am. She intimidates me, and I almost surely bore her.

All this, however, didn't particularly daunt me when I left the backwoods for my stint in civilization. I'd become accustomed to being alone. I could always find something to occupy my mind and hands, and when there was no one else to talk to, I could talk to myself. I'll admit that the first time I caught myself saying out loud, "Now let me see. I guess I'd better fill the water pails before it gets dark," I received a slight shock. I thought I was going woods queer. But I was reassured when I discovered that Alys Parsons, who also spends a great deal of time alone, talks to herself, too. It isn't a sign of anything except possibly the very slight barrier dividing thought from speech. It works in reverse just as well. There have been many occasions upon which I have been positive that I'd made some comment, when it turned out that I'd only thought it. It's only when you are constantly with others that the monitor in charge of preventing you from speaking your mind, with possible dire consequences, is on the job.

Anyhow, I had my plans all made for my first winter in Bridgewater. I was going to catch up on my reading, in which I was about fifteen years behind. In the woods, the only new books I had access to were those given me by pitying friends, a slim crop to be hoarded and read slowly, to make them last. When they were gone, I had to go cruising through the book shelves for something I liked well enough to re-read, or had forgotten sufficiently so that reading it again would seem like a new experience. Bridgewater has a public library, a feature I esteem far above the other public utilities of electricity and running water, snow removal, and fire and police protection. It isn't a very large library and not overburdened with funds, but at least it does have a constant trickle of the more important new books, as well as a good solid back-log of all those I had missed over the years. My world of escape from family problems, I thought, would be one long binge of reading.

It didn't work out quite that way. Oh, sure, I went to the library, all set to explain who I was and that I would like to take out a card. The minute I opened the door, I was back in my teens. The place looked just the same and smelled just the same, of floor-wax, old books, and steam heat. The same shabby old man sat dozing over a magazine in the Reading Room, and the same—or very similar—High School students whispered and giggled quietly near the card index as they pretended to do their home-work. The same Librarian sat at the desk and greeted me in the same old way: "Hello, Louise. How's your mother?" For all the emotion she showed, I might have been in only yesterday, instead of a decade and a half ago. And standing in front of the shelves where the more recent books are kept, right where I had left her fifteen years before, was Alice Folsom, who used to sit beside me in High School French.

"Hi, Louise," she said. "What's good to read? I've read everything here, and most of it's terrible. Pretty soon I'm going to have to write a book myself, just to have something decent to read."

"That's what I thought, too," I told her with absolute untruth. "That's why I'm in the business." Actually I'm constantly impressed with the excellence of the books other people write. Those who have never tried it themselves feel very free to criticize the writings of others. It's not as simple as it looks; and the simpler it looks, the harder it is to do, a principle that applies also to such things as figure skating, hitting C above high C, or making really good pie crust.

Alice returned the book she had been holding to the shelves and dusted her hands disdainfully. "I'm having a few people in on Election Night to listen to the returns, Louise. It's not really a party, but I'd love to have you drop in, if you'd like. Any time at all after dinner."

So I went to the Election Party, and that introduced me to— No, not a mad social whirl, but to a small group of congenial souls, some of whom I had known years ago, and some of whom I was meeting for the first time. So now every single day I see four or five persons, aside from my own family, with whom I am well enough acquainted to stop and engage in conversation, or to drive with out into the country, looking for apples or bittersweet. After my old life, when I saw a different face perhaps once in two or three weeks, this is indeed an embarrassment of riches.

It's also very confusing, and I'll tell you why. As I said, in the backwoods I knew very few people and saw almost nobody, because there were so very few of us to see and know. But we knew each other well. We had time to listen to each other, and to think about each other, so that we understood each other. Nothing anyone did, no matter how bizarre it might seem to an outsider, was particularly startling. Being thoroughly familiar not only with the circumstances leading up to the action, but also with the state of mind of the actor, we accepted the act as logical and inevitable. Moreover, people were always the same as when you saw them last, or, if their behavior deviated slightly from their norm, you were not surprised. You knew all about the money they'd just inherited, and expected them to be gayer than usual, or about the boat they'd just had destroyed by fire, and expected them to be slightly grim. It was a condition conducive to a state of social stability.

Here it's very different. People say and do the darndest things, with absolutely no apparent reason. The reasons must exist. I can't believe that a large part of the population acts constantly on irresponsible impulse. No, the reasons are there, all right; I just don't happen to know what they are, a fact that sets me to biting my nails with frustration. I like to be able to explain, if not to anticipate, aberrations in conduct. When I can't, I feel as though I were wandering around with my head in a burlap bag, stepping on toes, ramming my elbow into stomachs, and otherwise behaving uncouthly. It really mixes me up when I invite two women, inseparable, I had thought, to lunch, only to discover that they are not speaking to each other, and the next week find them all palsy-walsy among the cauliflowers in the First National Store. You just can't imagine how utterly bewildering people can be until you've been without them for fifteen years.

Alice Folsom, however, is one person I'm sure of finding exactly as I expect to find her. You see I know her very well and am familiar with the ups and downs of her emotional, physical, and material life. We spend a lot of time together, partly because we are congenial and partly because she, too, is a woman without a husband.

The position of the lone woman is a little bit difficult when she gets to be our age. We're very welcome at all the hen parties, but we're a slight embarrassment when the married couples foregather. Not that everyone isn't nice to us, but—if the dinner is to take place in a restaurant, who is going to pay our checks? Apparently it's unthinkable that we should pay our own; but then who is going to get stuck? Will they toss coins for us, or split us up? If the dinner is to take place at someone's home, either we unbalance the seating arrangement or else some poor suspicious soul is dragged in to even things up. He always has a slightly white-eyed look, like a spooky horse, as though he were being set upon the path to the altar much against his will. Since the altar doesn't interest either Alice or me in the slightest at this stage of the game, we find this extremely annoying.

Then there is the question of the very delicate line between coolness and over-friendliness that you must walk when you are around other women's husbands. Coolness is bad. It implies that you don't like Bill and are obliquely criticizing his wife's taste in life companions. But it's worse to find a topic of mutual interest to discuss at length with Bill, even if it is as unromantic a topic as the tendency of steel to crystalize under continuous vibration or the mechanics of making a contour map. I gather that such a conversation, carried on publicly and in normal speaking tones, can be and sometimes is open to misinterpretation as the first step in a campaign of husband stealing. If I had a husband who could be stolen that easily, I'd either let him go and good riddance, or I'd bone up on steel and maps myself. This sounds catty, but I do get tired of trying to act like a cross between a noble and aging St. Bernard and a particularly young and ingenuous Girl Scout.

The upshot of this is that Alice and I find ourselves by personal preference and tacit public consent left to our own simple devices on those occasions when our married friends are out howling with their husbands. If this makes us sound pretty pathetic, I'm not only sorry; I'm indignant. We aren't pathetic at all. We have a very good time, thank you. We have such a good time, in fact, that an acquaintance-from-kindergarten of mine, a rather grim and serious-minded lady, called me up the other day about it.

After a little hemming and hawing, she said in a this-hurts-me-more-than-it-does-you tone, "Louise, I think you ought to know that you and Alice Folsom are being talked about."

I indulged in a lightning-like mental review of our activities during the past month or so, and as far as I could determine, our slates were antiseptically clean. "What are we supposed to have done now?" I asked, more curious than hurt or disturbed.

"Well, I heard—and I'm not going to tell you where I heard it, so it'll do you no good to ask me—that you were all over town acting like summer people."

I hooted, in spite of the gravity of this indictment; and when I had my regrettable levity under control, I asked, "Just exactly what were we doing, or didn't you find out?" I was interested in having catalogued for me the stigmata by which you recognize the genus summer people.

She'd found out, all right. She had the charges down in specific, damning detail. First, we'd come reeling out of the Five and Ten Cent Store laughing so hard that we'd had to lean against the side of the building. Then, separated by the stream of traffic at the intersection, we'd shouted from corner to corner to each other as to our immediate individual destinations. (I was going to the Post Office and Alice was going to the News Store, my friend on the telephone told me circumstantially.) A short time later, we'd sat in my car and smoked, while apparently going over our shopping lists. And last, and worst, we'd been making faces through the A&P window at people outside. And what, her tight-lipped silence demanded, did I have to say to that?

What could I say to it, except that her informant was a remarkably accurate reporter? We were guilty as charged, even to the making of faces through the window of the Great Atlantic and Pacific Tea Company. Rufus, going by on the sidewalk, had seen us inside and made his Chimpanzee Face at us. Naturally, I'd crossed my eyes and stuck out my tongue at him. Any woman of spirit would have done the same. One thing led to another, with Alice pitching in on my side with her Idiot Child Face, until the three of us simultaneously tired of the game and went about our respective businesses. I'll admit we were noisy and silly and indulging in conduct unbecoming to our age, sex, and station in life; but we were harming no one and having fun, so what the heck? Summer people indeed!

When I first came here, Bridgewater had a moving picture theater, which has since died of malnutrition. During my years in the woods I never went to the movies; and by never I mean never, not ever, period. I couldn't have, if I'd wanted to. So, far from being one of these addicts who goes to the movies every time the show changes, just to be going to the movies, I went only when I was quite sure that I wanted to see the picture. Alice shares this attitude with me, so about four times a winter we'd go to the early evening show, a great treat for both us cloistered souls. I'll have to admit that half our fun lay in picking the picture to pieces afterward. Movies are always so much less good than they ought to be, it seems to me. Usually we started the autopsy before we were well outside the theater, to the dismay of Mr. Murphy, the manager. "Shh!" he'd say desperately. "Can't you wait until you get home? You're ruining my business." And he'd cast a hunted look at the handful of prospective customers around the ticket booth.

Finally he went further. One rainy spring afternoon when we'd decided to go to the matinee and bustled up with our quarters clutched in our hot little fists, he intercepted us on the sidewalk. "Don't sell 'em tickets, Bea," he instructed the ticket girl.

"What do you mean, don't sell us tickets?" Alice demanded. "Are we Typhoid Marys or something?"

"No, but you won't like the show. I know what you two like, and you won't like this."

"Why, I never heard of such a thing! You're a fine businessman, turning away cash customers!" I exclaimed. "Why not let us judge for ourselves?"

Mr. Murphy said earnestly, "Because I know you won't like it, and you'll come out and belly-ache to me, besides going all over town telling your friends that the picture is brutal. I'm trying to make it good for myself all around."

So we took him at his word and spent our quarters on flower seeds instead. For entertainment in place of the brutal picture, we stopped at the intersection and talked with the Chief of Police, whom we have both known from the cradle and who was keeping a paternal eye on the traffic and pedestrians at this busiest spot in town. We'd been wanting to clear up a few matters with him ever since we'd spent a fascinating afternoon reading the latest Town Report.

Bridgewater, like most New England towns and very likely towns elsewhere, publishes each year a report on those things that should be of interest to the conscientious citizen. The finances of the town are dealt with in detail, and the heads of the various departments—Fire, School, Water, Street, Forestry—make their accountings to the taxpayers. But the sections Alice and I pore over most avidly are the Vital Statistics—you know, Marriages, Births, and Deaths—because I'm ashamed to say that we are not above a little finger-counting, if you know what I mean; and the report of the Police Department, which is far more intriguing and provocative actually than whether that Jimson girl had what is known politely as a seven-months' baby. The Police Report takes up several pages and lists every activity—every professional activity, that is—of the boys with the badges for the past year. It is the most tantalizing bit of printed matter that I've ever come across. What would you make of the bare notation, for example, "Horses reported lost, 7," and then on the next line, "Horses recovered, 6"? What became of that extra horse? Even more baffling is "Cows reported lost, 9," followed by "Cows recovered, 10." Did a cow wander in from Raynham? Or did a legitimate Bridgewater cow give birth during her absence?

Then there are crimes listed that I have never before had occasion to consider. "Stoning cats, 4," yes, maybe. But what about "Stoning train, 1"? Who'd want to throw stones at a train? Was it some infuriated commuter who arrived puffing and panting just too late to climb aboard, or just a hide-bound Tory that had become fed up with these here now modern innovations? But the crime that Alice and I wanted to have explained more fully was listed with stark simplicity as "Geese eating goldfish, 1."

"Oh, that. Oh, yes," said the Chief. "Woman way down South Street. She's got a lily pool in her garden that she keeps goldfish in, and the neighbor's geese got out and went over and started eating them, so she called us."

"You mean you had to go way down there just for that?" I asked. "Why didn't she just go out and chase them away herself with a broom?"

"Did you ever try to chase a goose or especially a big gander with a broom, Louise?" he inquired. "Those things can be pretty mean and nasty. Sure we went down. We had a heck of a time, too. Oh, well, all in the day's work," and he frowned ominously at a truck that had overshot the stop line. We decided tacitly not to ask him about "Riding pig, 1." He'd probably have an equally obvious explanation, and we preferred the wild joys of unhampered speculation.

Alice keeps house for her father, a gentleman of eighty-eight years, so we spend a lot of time pursuing our favorite occupation, plain talking, there, to keep him company. The Folsoms' is a fascinating house, with a beautiful fireplace in every room. It's over two hundred years old, and has a secret staircase, that dream of everybody's early childhood. It used to be owned many years ago by a Miss Bathya Holmes, a maiden lady of strong character, famous for once routing a thug who laid hands on her prim person by ordering in a quiet and frigid voice, "Desist! At once!" And he did desist, and at once, too, whether from astonishment or because he recognized a superior moral force I have no way of knowing. Miss Bathya has been gathered to her fathers long since; but Alice's sister Sylvia maintains stoutly that upon two occasions, when she was a young girl, she saw plainly in broad daylight the ghost of Miss Holmes, once sitting by the living-room fire, once coming down the long front stairway. While Sylvia is telling it, I am convinced, although when I am out from under the influence of her dramatic ability I find myself entertaining doubts. However, it's an interesting idea, and quite in keeping with the age and beauty of the house.

Our houses and yards occupy a great deal of Alice's and my time and thought. My house is old, too, about a hundred years, and as anyone who has lived in one knows, an old house is always in need of attention. Since we are both husbandless, we are the ones who have to run around with a hammer and piece of old board to patch up the bulkhead, slap a little paint on the pantry shelves, trim back the spirea, forsythia and syringa bushes in the fall, and soak off that terrible old oat-meal paper in the guest-room, in case the paper-hanger really does get around to coming next week. Consequently, much of our conversation deals with brands of paint, whether or not cold water paint is a satisfactory answer to wall problems, and what to do about crab grass in the lawn or moles among the tulip bulbs. We sound pretty settled and stodgy, and I guess we are; but these are things which interest us. I might just as well confess now that we also swap recipes, a form of entertainment that I once considered as the Absolute Low.

In fact, the more I consider this personal and private

life I was going to tell you about, this life into which I escape from my maternal obligations, the simpler and stupider it seems. Once in a while I recall with a feeling of slight dismay and some incredulity the list of things that I, at the age of eighteen, had intended to do long before I ever came within spitting distance of my present age. I was going to cross the Andes on foot, for one thing—why, I don't remember. I was also going around the world on a freighter, and at the present moment, all this well behind me, I should be either living on a ranch in New Zealand, homesteading in Alaska, or well settled-in on the Channel Islands. Well, I'm not. I'm right back where I started from, and it's too late to do much about it now, I'm afraid. If at eighteen I could have foreseen my present far from romantic situation as mother, housewife and wage-earner—in Bridgewater, of all places, whose dust I planned to shake from my feet as soon as feasible!—I should probably have become ill with chagrin. As things are, I don't mind my fate at all, a fact that would have seemed to that eighteen-year-older the final symptom of complete mental deterioration. To live this life would be bad enough, but not to rebel, not to mind— Well! How young and fiery-hearted we all were once.

The reason I don't mind is that I like people. I like to try to figure out what the basic structures of their lives are, what their relationships to each other are, why they seem to be happy or unhappy. I like to speculate on what is going on under the surface they present to the world. If they are cross-grained and bitter, I like to look for the reason—because no one, surely, deliberately decides to be that way. Only the disappointed or discontented or wretched are sour and disagreeable. Or if I find someone who seems to me to be having a miserable time, ridden with poverty or illness or condemned to a life of drudgery at some distasteful task, but still remains warm and friendly and out-giving, I like to try to discover upon what secret source of strength he is drawing. It's an absorbing study, and I have been for a long time without new material to work on. That's why I'm so engrossed in my magpie-like collecting of bits and scraps of information and in piecing them together in an attempt to form a design that makes sense. I said that people are confusing; but if you really look at them and listen to them and think about them, some sort of order begins to emerge from the confusion. Me, I like order.

This preoccupation with the affairs of others—call it nosiness, if you want to—can lead into pit-falls. For some time I have been titillated by a sudden and inexplicable intimacy between two women with whom I have a bare nodding—or head-yanking, as we call it in Maine—acquaintance. I'd see them in stores together, holding low-voiced conferences over the merchandise, or riding around together in each others' cars, or running into and out of each others' houses in an informal manner. I couldn't figure it out. As far as I could see, they didn't have a thing in common. I tried on for size the notion that the son of one was courting the daughter of the other, and a future family tie was being spun. It didn't fit, though. The son in question was twenty-four, a likely age, but the only daughter in the picture was six, and a brat at that. Then my mother made a chance remark yesterday, and the situation became crystal clear. The two women attend the same church and are working together this year on the big, pre-Christmas Church Fair. So much for my deep researches into the arcana of human nature. Let it be a lesson to me.

If I had lived here from childhood continuously, I would not have made that mistake. I'd have had at my tongue's end the religious affiliations of, as well as any other pertinent information about, almost everyone in town. But I would undoubtedly have been guilty of making mistakes of a much worse nature. Let me give you an example of what I mean.

I met at one charity tea or another a very pleasant woman with a good sense of humor. We did a certain amount of chit-chatting, and I liked and enjoyed her very much; so much in fact that I remarked the next day to a group of my older-established friends on what a nice and intelligent woman Mrs. Acres (not her name) was. I hoped I'd see her again, I said.

Everyone looked blank, so I went on to describe her. "Oh!" said one of my friends. "She means Jennie Blastic!" And everyone laughed pityingly at my lack of sophistication. "Why, you know who she was, Louise. She came from that no-account Blastic tribe down across the tracks. You ought to remember her. Her older brother was in our grade in grammar school—an awful oaf. Of course you remember her. She *had* to get married to Ed Acres."

"What do you mean, she *had* to get married to Ed Acres?" I asked, and was told for heaven's sake to be my age. "No, what I mean," I tried to explain, "is that her son is well over twenty, so all that must have been a long time ago; and she isn't responsible for the oafishness of her brother, is she? Or is she still—shall we say gay? She certainly doesn't look or act it."

Oh, no. She seemed to have settled down after her marriage and had brought her children up very well. But the fact still remained that she'd been one of Chowderhead Blastic's kid sisters, and she had had to get married. So after *all!* And *really,* Louise!

Now where I've lived for many years, we accept people at face value. This isn't because we're a bit more charitable or broadminded than the average citizen. We just happen to live under circumstances that make this attitude easy to maintain. There's no other side of the tracks there. There's nothing except the woods and the mountains and the lakes, for mile after lovely, lonely mile. Nobody—except Rufus—was born in that country. We all came from somewhere else, leaving behind us any youthful indiscretions or embarrassing family connections. What we know about each other is only what we choose to tell each other—and, of course, what we observe about each other. We're portraits without background to prejudice the viewer, at first; and the type of background that is slowly filled in over the years depends entirely upon the individual as he is now, not upon what he used to be or what his parents were before him. You make or break yourself, with no hindrance and no help, either, from the past. This is, I suppose, a condition that was prevalent in the days of the colonization of this nation, and a condition that must exist still on all frontiers. At any rate, it comes the nearest of anything I know about to the true democratic ideal and principle in practice. It's a demonstration of the concepts of equality and justice actually applied. It was easy for me to be fair in the backwoods, so I take no credit for it.

But you'd think, wouldn't you, that, having seen how happily such a system works out, I'd make a point of applying it as far as my own personal conduct goes, no matter where I live or what my friends think of the whole thing? I'm deeply ashamed and very much disturbed to say that I don't. I haven't the courage of my convictions, I guess. I still like Mrs. Acres, but I never have got to know her any better. Oh, we meet on the street and exchange the amenities, but that's as far as it goes. I tell myself that I'm too busy to make an opportunity to know her better, although I know perfectly well that we all find time to do the things we really want to do. The truth is that I have allowed myself to be influenced by the prejudices and opinions of others, to become blinded by the general haze of gossip and eye-brow raising. Mrs. Acres, I'm sure, gets along perfectly well without me, so I'm not doing her any great harm; the one I'm harming is myself, by letting myself be whittled down to this size.

When I first came back here to live, one of the commonest questions asked me was, "How does it seem to be back in Civilization, Louise?" I'd have to admit that I didn't know, I hadn't had time to find out yet.

There are still times in the winter when I think of Forest Lodge with the snow silently thickening on the roof and capping the smokeless fieldstone chimneys, while down below the empty rooms grow colder and colder and bleaker and bleaker; and then I am overcome with nostalgia. The river, steaming gently in the clear frigid air, is still tumbling down over the ledges, and the wind is tossing the crowns of the tall pines, and the shadow of the big rock by the back door is describing its slow arc from West to East as the low winter sun moves in its ancient course, and I'm not there. I was happy there, happier than I have ever been before or since, and it seems to me that if only I could go back——

But of course that is childish and ridiculous. You can never go back, and there is nothing so futile as trying to do so, nothing so foolish as wasting the fleeting present and entailing the uncertain future by a preoccupation with the past. You can remember the past with affection and plan for the future with hope; but the only time in which you can live is the present. My present happens to be laid here in Bridgewater, and if I sometimes feel like a woman from Mars, that is all to the good. It gives me perspective, which I hope I'll be wise enough to appreciate and employ. It lends richness and meaning to the tame little occupations which add up to The Private Life of the Rich Children's Mother.

CHAPTER SEVEN

Beach-head Established

LAST winter it came to my attention that, in spite of the fact that Bridgewater is only twenty miles from the ocean, my children had never been swimming in salt water. We were in Bridgewater only during the winter months, when swimming in the North Atlantic isn't very feasible; and as soon as spring came and school closed, we were always so a-fire to get to Maine and Forest Lodge that we couldn't take time out for anything. One thought led to another, and I ended convinced that every child should have a summer at the beach to remember, if it were at all possible to arrange. The kids were going to fight like steers when I broached this idea, I knew; and I myself felt a little old-fashioned—as we say in Maine when we mean vaguely depressed and unhappy—at the thought of a summer away from the north woods and lakes. But it seemed to me my duty as a parent at least to subject them to a change of vacation spots. It was time anyhow that they were apprised of the fundamental fact of life that there does exist a world beyond the borders of Maine, in which it is possible to have fun in summer, and that there are, living and having their being, other people and other things than Down-easters and pine trees. This conclusion reached, I set about finding a cottage to rent for the season.

This was a discouraging business. Of only one thing was I sure: this hypothetical cottage had to be smack on the beach. What's the point of going to the shore if you have to walk half a mile on a Tarvia road to swim, and see the ocean only as a distant glimpse of blue between a couple of shanties? There is no point in that at all. If we were going to the beach, we were going to the beach. Otherwise we'd call off all bets and go home to Maine. I started my search on Cape Cod.

But the Cape has changed since the olden days. It's popular and stylish now. Anything on the waterfront was much too expensive for me. Heck, anything a day's journey from the waterfront—if such a thing is possible on the Cape—was still too expensive. Besides, down there we'd have to dress up half the time. We are a family of non-dressers-up, as anyone who knows us will gladly testify, probably adding revolting details of the way we slop around in old clothes. It has to be a pretty good reason, like church, for example, to get us into our store clothes. The Cape being out, I was temporarily at a loss.

Then one blustery winter's afternoon, I drove my friend Alice Folsom down to Mattapoisett to call on her aunt, Miss Cannon of Cannon Street. More as routine than anything else, I unhopefully asked my hostess if she knew of any cottage thereabouts that I could rent. I knew it was a silly question.

"Why, yes," she said, and I almost toppled over dead in

the middle of her lovely old parlor. "Lydia Doren wants to rent her Angelica Point place, I think." I pulled myself together with some difficulty and began to ask questions. "Lydia's right across the street," Miss Cannon told me. "I'll go get her, and perhaps you can drive down to Angelica and see for yourself."

So that's what we did, and the upshot was that I rented the place on the spot, from Memorial Day until the first of October. It was just exactly what I'd had in mind, although even in my rosiest opium dreams I had never hoped for anything that met the specifications so perfectly.

Mattapoisett is on the west shore of Buzzards Bay, seven miles from the famous old whaling city and port of New Bedford. The name is retained from the Indian and means "Place of Resting"; and that is still a good, descriptive name for it. It is a peaceful little town, off the roaring main highway, with quiet, narrow streets, beautiful old houses, and a small, safe harbor. There are no chain stores or movies or juke joints. Up to the time I became a summer resident, my impression of the place, gained through occasional calls with Alice on her aunt, was one of fresh salt breezes, sunlight, sparkling water, old elms, and flowers. I never saw such consistently lovely flower gardens anywhere—not elaborate affairs, but just the plain, old-time door-yard variety. Of course everyone knows that the presence of a large body of water, like the Atlantic Ocean, has a stabilizing and moderating effect on the temperature, but that doesn't seem to be enough to account for the success that any fool in Mattapoisett seems to have with flowers. Not that I know any special fools in Mattapoisett, but *everyone* has a riot of bloom in the yard, and surely the population can't be 100% unsung

Luther Burbanks. Roses, pink and white and yellow and crimson, flower from April until November. Nasturtiums spill over walls onto the roadside, and dahlias droop their great velvet heads in stately rows. The colors are brighter and the growth more abandoned than seems quite decent in New England. In the fields and meadows outside the town proper, the wild flowers—the white daisies and the ox-eyed, the wild roses and lupin and loose-strife and arnica—blaze prodigally.

Angelica Point is a hook-shaped sand-spit about four miles by road from the village, at the east side of the entrance to the harbor. Down the middle of the spit runs a narrow road, stopping short at the last cottage, about halfway along the point. You can get a car over it, but it's no boulevard. It isn't worth while to put in a really first class road, since the southeasters of winter frequently roll the surf completely over the point, washing out any engineering projects that have been undertaken. Anyhow, the only traffic consists of the cars of the few families who summer on Angelica—less than a dozen—and delivery trucks. The seaward half of the point is a wild, uninhabited jungle of wind-distorted scrub trees, great rocks, and the overgrown foundation of a hurricane-destroyed house.

On the east side, in front of the handful of cottages, lies Buzzards Bay, with the channel of the Cape Cod Canal running down the middle; and out back, on the west side, is a shallow inlet called Pine Island Pond, although I don't know why. I thought that a pond was always fresh water, and this is salt; and there is no island at all in it, unless you want to count some clam flats which are exposed at low tide. I don't remember any outstanding pine tree, either, although there are specimens of the long-needled, scrubby variety more or less all over the countryside.

Lydia Doren told me rather apologetically that what I was going to see was really nothing but a beach shack. The first cottage they'd had on the site was really nice, she said; but it was swept away in the hurricane of 1938. The next one they built wasn't quite so elaborate, but it was still nice. That went out in the next hurricane, a few years later. They found the kitchen sink over across Pine Island Pond, up in the woods. Understandably daunted, this time she and her husband just picked up what pieces they could find and slapped them together again as best they could. At least, she said, it made a place to eat and sleep and come in out of the rain. I said that was really all you needed at the beach, preparing myself meanwhile for a tar-paper and tin monstrosity. Then we arrived at the shack.

It turned out to be a neat, low, L-shaped building, painted gray with faded-blue trim, and it was built with the ingenious space-employing economy of a ship. It looked small from the outside, but there was a large living-room with a Franklin stove, a good-sized bed-room, a kitchen with a dining alcove, and a bathroom. There were, believe it or not, four large closets and built-in dish shelves. I have never in my life had enough closet space, so that feature alone would have sold me. (Mr. Doren is an architect, and a good one, which accounts for this masterly planning.) There was running water and a white kitchen sink, slightly marred from its trip across Pine Island Pond, it's true, but large and serviceable, and high enough, thank the Lord. Being tall, I have horrible low-sink trouble. I don't mind washing dishes, but I do mind having my back broken while at the chore. There was an electric refrigerator, and electric lights situated so that you could actually use them, and not have to sit with your book at an awkward angle while you slowly went blind by the light of one drop bulb in the center of the room. Cots in the living room and dining alcove supplied extra sleeping quarters, their blue, ship-printed spreads relieving them of That Bed-room Look. The other furnishings were simple, attractive, and good, and no matter from what window you gazed, you had a view of water. In the angle of the L, sheltered from the wind but open to the sun, was a brick terrace with a rail around it, an ideal adjunct for drying bathing suits. Along the base of the building were narrow flower beds, and window boxes outside the kitchen and living room overlooked the terrace. There was, moreover, a row boat that went with the place.

I said, "Well!" I'd planned on being right on the beach. Here the ocean practically came in one door and went out the other. The terrace was twenty feet from the high tide line in front, and in back you had only to cross the road, and walk through a patch of salt grass and sea lavender to come to the Pond. The beach, I could see, was wonderful, sandy and gently shelving. There was no lawn to mow, and the shack was small enough so that even the laziest housekeeper (me) could sweep it from one end to the other, including corners, in ten minutes flat. Since I am very apt to be carried away with my enthusiasms, I looked about for a flaw. I could see none, so I muttered something about mosquitoes from the marshland near the pond, and the heat of summer out here on the open beach, with no trees for shade. Lydia assured me that it was always cool on Angelica, no matter which way the breeze blew. It always came across water, she said. And as for mosquitoes— What were they? Nobody had seen a mosquito for years, not since the mosquito control project had ditched and drained the swamp. I took all this with a grain of salt, for which I hereby apologize. She was absolutely right. We were never too hot, and we never saw a mosquito. So we completed the deal right then and there. Then all I had to do was wait out the months until Memorial Day.

It wasn't an easy waiting. As I had anticipated, the kids took a dim view. They wanted to go to Maine. They weren't going to like the beach, they said, with a stubborn set of jaws. I began to have doubts myself. If they'd made up their minds not to like it, of course they wouldn't. However, I bravely laid it on the line. "You're going to the shore. And that is that. So you'd better start liking the idea right now." This was bad psychology, I know, but I was sick and tired of fussing around with them. Only Parents get that way sometimes. Probably all parents do.

Memorial Day week-end was fortunately lovely, clear and balmy. We loaded our tons of duffle, the cat, the dog, and ourselves into the car and set out. We had everything we needed, I thought, except a bathing cap for Dinah and ear plugs for Rufus, who always gets his ears full of water when he swims. I thought I'd stop in Mattapoisett proper for them. It was too early in the season for inland stores to be carrying beach supplies. We drew up in front of the Village Shop on Water Street, and trailed in.

The woman in charge was leaning on a counter, chatting with a friend. They finished their conversation, while we waited. Then the proprietress moved over to us and asked if she could help us. I outlined briefly our simple wants, while the friend looked us over, taking in every detail of our costumes, from shabby loafers through rolled up dungarees and plaid shirts, to bare heads. *She* was wearing a pretty print dress and a hat. Then she looked out the window over the harbor and said to no one in particular, in a faraway voice to match the faraway expression in her eyes, "Hmm. I see The Season's started."

I did a very slow double-take, and my jaw dropped. Well, for crying out loud! The Season, indeed! Because for seventeen years *I* had been the Native, looking down my nose and smiling tolerantly at the Summer People, those silly coots who meant so well, but didn't really know which way was up. And *now*— Oh, well, I was off the reservation now, and having dished it out for so long, it behooved me to take it with good grace. I paid for my purchases with unaccustomed meekness.

Remember, now, we had lived for years in the forested mountains of western Maine, where all the lines of the scenery go up, leading the eye higher and higher from lake shore, to foot-hill, to the far, dim ranges. At Forest Lodge we were forever in a green, aromatic, whispering shade. The sun-light sifted down through the feathery tops of the spruce and fir; or we had to seek it on river bank or in the quiet clearings. The sky was a narrow blue tent, stretched tautly across the valleys from ridge to ridge and seen almost always through a lacy fret-work of branches. The earth—the mountains and the rivers and the tall-reaching trees—was the big thing.

It was different at the beach. We found that out on that first afternoon when, possessions stored away, we sat down to rest in the chairs on the terrace. The tide was almost out, and the bars and shallows showed clearly in the cove that lay in the curved arm of the point, before the water dropped off, a half a mile out, into the depths of Buzzards Bay. All the lines here were horizontal, the faded gold strip of the beach, the pale green and blue and lavender stripes in the cove, shading as the depths varied, the sharp stroke of indigo and purple where cove became bay. Flat on the horizon lay Falmouth, on Cape Cod, a dark slash in the eternal blue; and beyond it the faint, low, cloudy shapes of the Elizabeth Islands straggled southwest from Woods Hole—Nonomesset, Naushon, Pasque, Nashawena, and finally, so tentative as hardly to be credited, Cuttyhunk. The sun poured down on us, its light unbroken by leaf or twig, almost palpable in its clear intensity. And the sky was enormous, a great dome set on the insignificant saucer of the earth. I'd forgotten, if I'd ever known it, that there was so much sky, and that clouds could be so lovely, drifting up over Falmouth and marching, tall pillars and towers of cream and rose, across the deep blue vault. We just sat there and stared, while the sun sank slowly behind us, and the tide turned, and all the colors shifted and changed before our enchanted eyes.

Then, just as I was thinking about gathering myself together and preparing supper, a three-master under full sail came into sight from around Point Connett, on our left. She was moving along slowly, heeling a little under the breeze, her sails pink in the westering sun. Every detail of her deck and rigging was sharp and clear in the limpid air, so that she seemed almost like a painted ship against a painted background of blue water and distant, violet shore.

"Oh, Mummy," Dinah sighed, "I feel exactly as though I were living in a comic book!"

I snapped out of my mellow mood fast. Here I'd gone to untold trouble and expense to arrange a nice summer for those ungrateful brats, and what thanks did I get? None at all. Worse than none. (I was reacting like a parent, you'll observe.) Living in a comic book, forsooth! Comic books, so-called, are the bane of my existence. I used to forbid my kids to buy them or bring them into the house, until I chanced upon them one day leaning comfortably against a counter in the Five and Ten with their feet crossed, having a free read for themselves. Since this was obviously a form of cheating, if not stealing, which I felt sure the manager of the store would view with disapproval, I did break down to the extent of letting them buy a few once in a while. I know when I'm licked. All they needed was a few. As any parent knows, a lively traffic in comic books exists among the members of the grade school set. Given ten, say, even an indifferently smart operator can swap and juggle them around among his peers until he has read a hundred or more.

Annoyed as I was on this occasion, I managed to say with a false, sugary sweetness that I was far from feeling, "What do you mean, dear?"

"Oh, you know, Ma. Like—well, like all this isn't real; like it was something made up," Dinah explained confusedly.

What she meant, of course, was that she felt as though she were living in a fairy tale. At least, that's how my generation would have phrased it, corny goons that we were. I got over my mad and decided to have chocolate milk-shakes instead of just plain milk for supper, as a reward to her for this back-handed statement of approval.

After supper we planted our garden. I had decided weeks before that I was not going to be the only soul in Mattapoisett without a riot of bloom in her yard, so I'd bought half a bushel, more or less, of nasturtium seeds, which experience had taught me were pretty fool-proof. I discovered during the necessary loosening of the earth that the soil in the gardens was not sand, but good rich loam that must have been transported. This augured well, so we simply stuffed the border beds, the window boxes, and the wooden tub on the front steps with the things, being very careful about our rows and spacings. Then, feeling snugly installed, we whistled to Caro, the dog, and went for a walk, clear down to the end of the road. No one else had moved in yet, so we had a wonderful time, peering in the windows of unoccupied cottages and commenting on the furnishings.

When we got back, dusk was turning into dark, and we didn't at first see the young man in overalls knocking the last crumbs of soil from a series of seedling flats. Mrs. Doren had sent him down, he explained, to put in some petunia plants; and sure enough, the beds, thoroughly spaded, were full of sturdy little transplantings. I thanked him kindly, refraining from comment on my sabotaged nasturtiums. Maybe they wouldn't have come up anyhow, I thought; or if they had, maybe cut-worms or damping-off would have killed them. A petunia in the hand (or bed) was worth, *et cetera.*

But I guess there is something about Mattapoisett air, at that. By the first of July, I had quite a garden. Every nasturtium seed had come up at least twice, although not in the ordered ranks in which we had planted them. The young man with the spading fork had fixed that. They were all over the place, and they and the petunias fought a summer long battle for supremacy. It was a draw, but the results were good, from my viewpoint, if rather gaudy. Riot was the word for it, all right, with vivid orange, purple, scarlet, and magenta all screaming at each other.

These short week-ends at the shore before school closed, I had decided, with an uncharacteristic attempt at long range planning, would be a sort of breaking-in process. We'd get everything organized and simplified, so that when summer came and we moved down for good, we could get away with as little work as possible. When we had guests—and the bed situation allowed for only one at a time—everything would roll as smoothly as though a butler, cook, up-stairs girl, and yard-man were in residence, ministering to our every whim, while we sat around apparently not lifting a finger. We aren't really allergic to work, but we don't precisely love it for its own fair sake alone. We'd come to the shore to have fun; and I did not feel that laboring over a hot stove, or spending hours wielding a dry mop or rubbing my knuckles raw on a washboard would contribute to this end. Anyhow, I was supposed to be finishing a book, and the less time I was forced to spend on household chores, the more time I'd have to devote to my masterpiece.

The three basic needs of man, I once learned in a course I took, are food, shelter, and clothing. I didn't have to worry about shelter. I'd paid my rent, and if the roof blew off, that was the Dorens' headache. That left only food and clothing. I'd foresightedly invested in two bathing suits apiece, so we'd each always have a dry spare. I thought I'd wait and see what the Angelicans considered proper wear, before indulging in a buying spree of possibly unsuitable clothing. It was a good thing that I did, because it turned out that we seldom wore anything except the bathing suits. We put them on in the morning when we arose, covered them sketchily with shirts when we had to go into the village, let them dry on us in the hot sun after each of our two-dozen-a-day swims, and took them off only when we were ready for bed. When we went into the village, we did put on loafers or sneakers, as a further sop to conventionality. Otherwise we went barefoot from dawn right through until the next dawn. I was told that this would ruin our feet, or at least stretch them so that we'd all have to move into Size 14's, come fall. It didn't. Our feet were never so healthy, and I'm still wearing comfortably my winter-before-last's best and only pumps. And by the middle of August I could light a match on the soul of my foot. I'm not sure that this is a parlor trick to arouse envy in the breasts of the respectable matrons of my acquaintance, but it sure as shooting startles the living daylights out of most beholders.

That took care of clothing, and saved me time, trouble, money, and laundering. Short of growing coats of fur, like the dog and Cisco, the cat, I don't see how that problem could have been made any simpler.

So I had only the food situation to worry about. I rather like to cook, *if*—and it's a big if—I have proper utensils, proper ingredients, *and*—and it's a big *and*—a good stove that I can trust, with an easily regulated oven and a large top, varying in temperature from almost red hot at the front to luke-warm way back at the rear. In short, I like a wood-burning range. You can have your fancy gas and electric numbers. Me, I like a wood range, *if*—here we go again—I have a woodshed full of the right kinds of wood: tinder dry for a quick heat, year-old for a standard baking, and some nice this year's chunks—only in Maine we call them junks—of nearly green wood for a slow, steady, long-holding fire. At the shore I had an electric plate and a very good two-burner oil stove, if any oil stove can be called good. I had no oven at all, which cramped my style considerably, since I stick everything I can into the oven.

I could get breakfast easily enough under these no-proper-stove conditions. All we have in summer anyhow is fruit juice, dry cereal, egg on toast, and coffee or milk. Lunch at our house is a movable feast, consisting of whatever you want to drink, sandwiches which you'll make yourself whenever you feel like eating, using for fillings anything you can find in the refrigerator, and fruit or candy bars. You'll clean up after yourself, too, or have me to deal with. But dinner—there was where the rub came. Since we were having only one formal meal a day, really, it had to be good, with meat and potatoes, vegetables, a salad, and a real dessert. And how could I accomplish this with my measley little facilities? Roasts, the backbone of my weekly planning, were out. I had no oven. I'd have to lean back on chops and steaks, with occasional pot roasts, stews, or boiled dinners. And supposing I did get all this cooked and managed to keep it hot, how was I going to serve it? There were plenty of dishes, and very handsome they were. The table in the dining alcove was pretty handsome, too, a tavern type with a waxed surface. We ate elegantly off the bare boards; perish forbid I should involve myself with table cloths that had to be laundered. But there just wasn't room enough on it for dinner plates, salad plates, water glasses, milk glasses, coffee cups and saucers, and incidental relish dishes and bread plates and a center piece for more than three. Even if I kept the center piece modest, which I did, using an arrangement of shells instead of non-existent-at-the-moment flowers, still I had no area for a place setting for the not impossible guest.

Even so, I asked Alice Folsom down to spend one of these trial spin week-ends. I've known her all my life, so she didn't really count as a guest. And the children simply adore "Miss Folsom."— Am I old-fashioned? (This is a footnote.) I guess it's modern for children to bandy about Christian names when addressing their elders, but I still don't like it. My children will address my friends formally and respectfully, or else. (End of footnote.)

I'd secured some steak, and it looked good. I was organizing the dinner routine, bustling about the kitchen with a handful of silver, when Alice wandered in from the beach, where she'd been introducing my hill-billy off-spring to various types of marine life. She'd spent all her childhood summers with her Aunt Alice Cannon, so knew about things like horse-shoe crabs and razor clams, closed books to us.

"Steak!" she exclaimed, eyes glinting. "Oh, boy! Doesn't it look out of this world!"

"Yeah," I agreed. "I wish I could broil it, but I'm afraid it'll have to be fried. You can't broil on an oil stove, can you?"

"No." She thought the matter over. "Didn't I see an old oven shelf somewhere? Why can't we build a fire-place on the beach out front? All we need is the shelf for a grate, and some flat rocks. And a good strong back, like Rufus'."

I seized on the idea enthusiastically. You can be much less stylish on a cook-out than you can indoors. Everybody can cook his own dinner to taste, and if the steak is overdone, there is no one to blame but himself. All the work is divided in a way that isn't possible in a small kitchen, where even two people get in each other's way.

"I know where there are some elegant stones," I said, "not very far from here, either." And I did. On our first evening's walk down the point, we'd passed the ruined foundations of a house that had been swept away by one of the hurricanes, and hadn't been rebuilt. I put the steak back into the refrigerator and yelled for Rufus. Dinner was going to be a little late, but who cared?

We built the fire-place about twenty feet off the terrace. It looked a little amateurish, but it worked beautifully. We used the bottom of the over-turned boat for a serving table, and sat either on the ground or in chairs brought down from the terrace. All the dishes and silver and food was piled on trays and brought out in two short trips. I heated the frozen vegetables and made the coffee in the kitchen, bringing the pots and kettles out and arranging them around the edge of the grate to keep warm. Everybody helped himself when he was ready, saving a lot of trouble and dishes. And of course there was the further advantage of having a picnic in our own front yard, instead of miles away: if we forgot the salt, it was only a matter of half a minute to run into the house and get it.

As we lolled on the sand in the twilight, pleasantly stuffed with steak, and watched the lights of occasional freighters passing through the Canal, where the East Cleveland Ledge Lighthouse blinked steadfastly, I decided that we'd do a lot of eating outdoors this summer.

Everything was now under control in the departments of food, clothing, and shelter. We'd have a nice, quiet, peaceful summer, and I'd not only finish the book I was working on, but I might even start another, or at any rate, write some short stories. Then we'd take a lot of trips to the many places of interest so near us. We might as well make the most of our opportunities, I thought; and anyhow, there would certainly be times when we'd want a change of scenery and a little excitement in our lives.

Yes, we were all set and ready to roll.

CHAPTER EIGHT

The Visiting Firemen

AT least, that's what I thought, fool that I was. Oh, we rolled all right, but not always in the directions I had planned. It turned out that there were several factors that I had failed to take into consideration while prefabricating this nice, quiet, industrious vacation on the sands of the sea.

For one, I had forgotten that while the theory is that writing is nice work if you can get it—since you are your own boss, carry your business around in your head, and so can work anywhere at any time—in practice it doesn't quite pan out that way. Sure, if you don't like where you are, there's nothing to prevent your going somewhere else to finish your masterpiece. But writers as a class have two traits in common: (1) They'd rather do almost anything than sit down and write, snatching at any slim excuse to put off the evil hour when they have to face that sickeningly blank sheet of paper; and (2) They are almost pathologically curious about the world and people around them. Put a writer down in new surroundings, and he acts like a cat in a strange garret. He prowls and noses. He's fidgety and nervous. He can't settle down to work until he has become so completely familiar with his environment that it no longer has any surprises or much interest for him. I am no exception. I might as well admit right now that far from starting a new book, I never wrote one word on my old one until after Labor Day, and then only because my agent and editor became violently restive.

Naturally my typewriter was set up permanently in a corner of the living-room, with my unfinished manuscript beside it. It lent a lot of atmosphere. But the only times I ever touched either was to move it to provide a corner on which a caller could set down a glass of Coke, or to furnish a large enough surface for the flat drying of a piece of sea-weed. So we will say no more at all about the immense professional strides I made that summer.

Remember those interesting trips we were going to take? Well, during the month of July, I never got further afield than the village, four miles away, simply because there was too much to see and do and learn within this radius. After the contretemps in the Village Shop, I decided that we might just as well give up trying to pose as Natives. We'd admit quite freely that we were Summer People, Idiot Boy Class, and didn't know nutt'n, as the kids say. The Lord knows, this was the simple truth.

Take for example my dealings with Mr. Henshaw. Mr. Henshaw is the man who runs the fish market in the village. He conducts his business in a shack out on Long Wharf, just at the foot of Cannon Street. He buys his wares from the fishing boats as they come in to unload, popping the lobsters into tanks of running salt water, slapping the fish onto ice, and storing the shell-fish in the ice house. Since his stock is still gasping for life when you buy it, it leaves nothing to be desired for freshness and quality. But you see, I know nothing about buying fish. In the woods we either catch them or eat meat. Or settle for a can of tuna.

So the first time I went into Mr. Henshaw's place of business, I said, "I am Mrs. Rich, Mrs. Doren's tenant on Angelica. We are down here for the summer, and we've never been to the beach before. I'd like to buy some lobsters, but I don't know how to pick them out or how to cook them. Will you help me?"

Mr. Henshaw looks like a Yankee, which he is. He has the thin, intelligent face and the deliberate, independent manner with which I am familiar from my years in Maine; and by birthright, too, since I am a Yankee, although unfortunately not thin, nor sometimes too intelligent. He looked at me, the kind of look I understand, combining tolerance, slight amusement, and a willingness to please within reasonable limits, with a cynical conviction that most people, and especially most women, are fools.

"Well, we'll see what we can do," he said, and led me, trailed by Rufus and Dinah, over to the lobster tanks. "How many do you want and what size?"

I said I wanted three, one for each of us, and I didn't know what size. That was where he was supposed to help me. He hauled out a thrashing green crustacean, with claws neatly wedged, and said he guessed that would be about right. A little over a pound a-piece. Three this size, Mrs. Rich?

I said yes, I guessed so; and there we ran into difficulty.

Rufus announced flatly that if I thought he was going to eat one of those things, I was bats. He'd rather have hamburg.

"Me, too, son," Mr. Henshaw said, spoiling a sale with fine prodigal honesty. "Two, then, Mrs. Rich?"

Again I said yes, I guessed so; because anyhow, hamburg was cheaper than lobster, if that was how Rufus wanted it. Then Dinah put in her little oar. She wanted a lobster to eat, since she'd never had one and unlike her brother has a scientific curiosity; but she also wanted one for a pet. So, Ma, let's get three.

"Dinah," I said gently, "I don't think a lobster would make a very good pet. I don't know, but I don't think—"

"Yes, it would, if I loved it enough. If no one else fed it? If I took it to bed with me? Gee, Ma, Rufus had a skunk for a pet and you didn't say anything. If he could have a skunk, why can't I have a lobster? Aw, come on, Ma!"

I appealed to Mr. Henshaw, who was listening to this exchange with a long-suffering expression. "Mr. Henshaw, would you recommend a lobster as a pet?"

He smiled slightly. "Not exactly. Anyhow, you've got a dog and a cat." How he came by this information I don't know, but having lived in small towns most of my life, I have a fair idea. "You don't need a lobster. Two, then, Mrs. Rich?"

I said yes, two; and how did one cook them? He told me, and we went out with our purchase. Dinah's under lip stuck out so far that you could play solitaire on it. I felt like removing the wedges from the claws and letting her take the darn thing to bed with her. That would teach her. Instead I went back to ask where the nearest purveyor of hamburg was. It turned out to be E. A. Walsh, on Church Street, who, Mr. Henshaw told me, carried Everything.

This proved to be not entirely accurate, but near enough as doesn't matter. He carried everything that I, or almost anyone else, would want, from hip-boots to domestic champagne. It's a wonderful store. I, as a connoisseur of General Stores from way-back, say so. The store is in a rather tumble-down building, covering roughly half an acre, with narrow passages for the customers, the rest of the space being taken up by the stock. If you don't see what you want, you ask for it. Mr. Walsh, his kind, round face thoughtful, will scratch his ear.

"Yeah, we've got some of that around here some place. Guess we haven't got around to shelving it yet. Bob,"—Bob is his clerk—"look under those cartons of Rinso. See'f you can find some of those ripe olives for Mrs. Rich." In all my subsequent visits to the emporium of E. A. Walsh, I never saw any umbrella stands, Venetian blinds, or ballet slippers. But I never asked for them, so how do I know? Very likely he'd have been able to produce. I later heard of a store on Martha's Vineyard which stated on its sign, "We Carry Almost Everything." That leaves some leeway and inspires confidence by its conservatism. But I'll bet they haven't any better stock than Walsh of Mattapoisett.

Another thing I'd forgotten, since I had lived so long in Maine without any next-door ones, was how neighborly neighbors can be. I was the baby of the Angelica family, so to speak—baby not in years, let me hasten to add, but in period of residence. This was my first experience, while everyone else had been coming back season after season.

They all loved the place, and they wanted Baby to love it, too. So they all rallied around with help and advice.

Ruth Correia, for example, the mother of Don and Trudy—who are almost exactly the ages of Rufus and Dinah, and wasn't that a break!—fixed me up with the milkman, the laundryman, the fruitman, the mailman, and the baker. Moreover, every Friday when she went to New Bedford to do her week-end shopping, she took my list along, too. Since I don't especially like to do even my own shopping, let alone other people's, I thought this was darn nice of her.

Then there were the Campbells, four cottages along the beach. Mr. Campbell taught Rufus about quahoging. The quahog is a type of bivalve, fairly common along the Atlantic seaboard. The half-grown ones are commonly called cherrystone or little-neck clams, and are, I think, delicious eaten raw. The full grown ones are apt to be tough, but they make wonderful chowders. Most of the huge, ancient shell heaps left by the Indians all along the coast consist of quahog shells; and the famous purple wampum, which is the best and most valuable wampum, was made from the purple edges of the valve. I don't manufacture wampum, but I do use the larger shells for ash-trays. They're very successful, and you don't have to wash them. When they get dirty, you throw them away and get some more. Mr. Campbell taught me to open them, quite a trick, involving the use of a short, thick knife, and a constant danger of cutting off a finger.

In order to capture these succulent morsels, you wait until, as Dinah in her first ignorance told me, "the ocean is dead tired." She meant you wait for dead low tide, but never having heard of tides where she came from, she was a bit confused by Mr. Campbell's explanation. When the tide is low, then, you put on your oldest bathing suit and a pair of old shoes or sneakers, so you won't cut your feet, and set out, armed with the proper equipment, a long-handled, long-tined rake, and a wire basket. In Mattapoisett the best place to go is Pine Island Pond, and to get there you have to struggle through a marsh, with mud half-way to your knees. Once arrived, you stand in mud and water up to your knees or more, and claw around blindly with your rake in the muck. When you feel something like a small stone, you haul it up quickly, and if it's a quahog, you put it into your basket. If it's a scallop you throw it back, since scalloping isn't legal in the summer. The sun is usually blistering hot out on the flats, and the stench arising from the mud is inclined to be a bit high, but the results are worth the discomfort and trouble. Quahoging is not my favorite occupation, but Rufus became so enamoured of the sport that he'd go without even being ordered to; so we were kept well supplied all summer.

There was another delightful surprise in store for me in Mattapoisett. Twenty-five years or so ago I had a very good friend, Bea Kershaw, with whom I taught school in New Hampshire—my first job, in fact. We had a lot of fun together. We even went to Europe together one summer. Then we lost track of each other. You know how it is: we moved on to different jobs, got married, all that sort of thing. And now, to my great joy, she turned up again, this time as a Dr. Kershaw, a pediatrician, married to a Dr. Gardner, a psychiatrist, and mother of two girls, Ruth and Mary, just about Dinah's age. The Gardners had a cottage at Mattapoisett at The Cedars, a mile or two from us. I was glad of this for two reasons. I'd always liked her, and I found that she hadn't changed at all; and—as is not always the case with one's friends—I liked her husband, whom I had never met before. In addition to that, what could be handier than having a good pediatrician and a good psychiatrist on tap? It gave me a sense of great security. Now the kids could go right ahead and pick up viruses, and I could crack under the strain of adjusting to a new environment. Everything was taken care of; and possibly because that was the case, none of us developed anything at all untoward.

And George Gardner was such a comfort to me. He was writing his next book, too. We'd meet in shops and mutter to each other out of the corners of our mouths, "How's your book coming?"

The answer was always, "Oh, shut up! The same as yours."

All summer long I never saw him in anything except shorts or bathing trunks, sneakers, and a duck-billed cap; so it was a great shock to me when I attended a very erudite lecture he gave this winter to find that the man actually did own a very handsome suit and polished shoes. I almost didn't know him.

To make things simple in my life, I seem to have collected a list of women friends a large percentage of whom are named Alice. There are Alice Folsom, Alice Miller, and Alys (pronounced Alice) Parsons. To further complicate matters, my only sister's name is Alice. My sister, Alice Hoke, was coming to spend her vacation with us, and we thought it would be pleasant if her and Alice Folsom's vacations coincided, since we'd all grown up together. This could easily be arranged by having Alice

Folsom sleep at her Aunt Alice's. (Lord, another one!) We'd collect her daily before breakfast, she'd spend the day on the beach with us, and we'd return her at bedtime.

My sister was coming from New York by plane, which meant we'd meet her at the New Bedford airport at 10:30 a.m. All the way there I lectured the kids on Poor Auntie, let's give her a nice quiet vacation, she works so hard, she needs a rest. This developed into quite a long dissertation, since I got lost three times in trying to find the port. Remember, I'd been confining my explorations to my own backyard, more or less, and this was the first time I'd ventured into foreign and possibly hostile territory. We were a little late, but the plane was a little later, luckily. We drove back, everybody being quiet and good, so that Auntie could rest.

Back on Angelica, we spent a tranquil afternoon sunning and swimming and catching up on each others' gossip. I had planned, in order to celebrate my sister's arrival and to impress her with the joys of sea-side living, to have a lobster cook-out dinner; so as the sun sank behind us over Neds Point Light, I hounded Rufus into building a fire, told Dinah to take the terrace chairs and beach blankets down by the fire-place, and went inside to organize the food. Alice Folsom was thoroughly broken in to the cook-out routine—heck, she had originated it, back in June—so she had charge of the trays of silver and dishes. Poor Tired Auntie didn't have to do anything tonight. She could have the Guest Treatment for a while, at least.

I started the coffee on the oil-stove, tossed a green salad, assured myself that the large kettle of sea water on Rufus'

The lobsters went berserk. They thrashed in every direction and started climbing out again. My sister shrieked and tried vainly to clap on the cover.

fire was coming along nicely to a boil, and took from the refrigerator four of Mr. Henshaw's Finest and six hot-dogs for Rufus. At this point my sister came in and asked, "Isn't there *something* I can do? I feel like a bum loafing around while all of you are working."

"Well, if you want to," I said, "you can dump these lobsters into the kettle. The water's boiling. Just tip up the bag and slide them in and put the cover back on." She looked into the bag, where the lobsters were either sleeping or sulking with their claws all folded in, said sure, that was simple enough, and departed with them. I followed just in time to see her tilt the bag and dump the lobsters into the boiling water, as I had told her to do.

They went berserk. They thrashed in every direction and started climbing out again. My sister shrieked and tried vainly to clap on the cover. Mrs. Thompson shouted from the porch next door, "Quick. Put a stone on the cover!" Mr. Friedman, next door on the other side, came dashing up with a broken oar, and began poking them in as fast as they climbed out. Alice Folsom howled, "Don't tip over that pan of melted butter! Butter costs money!" The children danced around, screaming insanely; the dog barked; Ruth Correia, two doors away, called, "Want a larger kettle? You can have mine"; and an unidentified man who happened to be passing on the road tore around the corner of the cottage demanding, "What's the matter, what's the matter?"

When order had been restored, and the captains and the kings had departed, my sister asked a bit diffidently, "When you cook lobsters here, does it *always* turn into a combined riot and community project?"

Alice Folsom said, "Dear. Didn't you know? This is special. We are having a *quiet* dinner to-night, because Aunt Alice needs a rest."

I couldn't think of anything biting enough to say, so I gave her a dirty look and went into the kitchen to get the coffee and salad. Quiet or not, it was a good dinner. Outdoors is the place to eat lobster, and a bathing suit is the costume. You can crack claws between clean, sea-washed stones and dribble butter to your heart's content. You can throw the shells into the fire, use the ocean as a finger bowl, and, when you can't eat another mouthful, lie back on the sand and watch the stars come out one by one, while the moon swings low over Falmouth.

At nine o'clock Alice Folsom said she'd better be getting along, as her aunt went to bed fairly early. We drove her up to Cannon Street and left her outside her aunt's door. "Sleep well," she said to my sister sardonically.

"Now what do you mean by that?" I demanded. "I don't like your tone."

"We-ell. Nothing *much*. Only, Hoke, you'd better keep your door closed."

"If you're thinking of the night the dog jumped onto your bed and scared the daylights out of you, you can stop worrying. He stays outside nights now," I told her haughtily.

"And if you have ear-plugs, Alice—" my pal Folsom began again.

"Now stop," I said. "That night the kids both got to hollering in their sleep was an exception. They haven't done it since."

La Folsom shrugged and spread her hands expressively. "All right, all right. I was only trying to be helpful. You want Alice to have a nice quiet vacation, didn't you say? I was just trying—"

I slammed the car into gear. "Good *night!* I'll come get you around eight to-morrow morning."

We went home to bed.

At about three o'clock in the morning I was awakened by the agonized wailing of the cat. I am frankly not a cat lover, as I consider cats self-centered, egotistical, selfish, and smug. Did you ever hear of a cat's voluntarily sacrificing his comfort for any consideration? No. Does a cat come to you with tears in his eyes, offering sympathy, when you feel ill or sad? Certainly not. He comes yowling around wanting to know why in Hades you haven't prepared his lunch, and it had better be something more appetizing than that stuff you put out yesterday, and if you feel lousy, that's your tough luck. But Dinah adores cats, so I put up with them. We've had a long series, starting with Blue (because he was yellow), down through the years to our present incumbent, Cisco Kid (because of a radio program).

Cisco is, much as it hurts me to say so, very handsome; and he knows it. He's a blue-gray tiger, part angora, with a white breast and a full, beautiful plume of a tail. He swells around and I could kill him. After all, who runs this ranch, presumably? The answer should be Louise, but I'm afraid it's Cisco. However, out of respect for my daughter's feelings, I adopt a fairly forbearing attitude, confining myself to muttered imprecations when he twines around my feet and almost knocks me flat while I'm preparing a meal, and to giving him a shove with my foot when he hesitates in the screen door that I'm holding open for him while he makes up his mind, instead of the solid boot that he's asking for.

I dragged myself out of bed. *Now* what ailed that damn cat? Probably someone had inadvertently shut him into a closet, and now he wanted out. I started walking around saying softly, in order not to wake up the kids and Poor Tired Auntie, "Kitty, kitty, kitty," to help me locate him. The cottage is small, as I have said, with no sound-proofing whatsoever. Everywhere I went, the crying went with me, never getting either louder or softer. I looked in all the closets, creeping like a mouse into Alice's room for the purpose, and peered under all the beds. As I was halfway under Rufus' bed, he said loudly, "What's the matter?"

"Shhh!" I hissed like a viper. "I'm looking for the cat. Go to sleep."

"Oh." It wasn't his cat, so he went back to sleep.

But with a mother's instinct, Dinah sat bolt up-right and demanded, "What's the matter with my cat?"

"Shhh!" I hissed again. "I don't know. I'm trying to find him."

She jumped out of bed, knocking over a light chair, and helped me hunt. He wasn't anywhere in the house, although his voice followed us everywhere. By this time I'd decided that he'd been maimed while on his usual nocturnal foray, and had dragged himself home to die. He was probably under the house, and it was up to me to find him and give him what succor I could. While I don't like cats, I am not a sadist, after all, and nothing under my care is going to die untended. I found a flashlight, and with Dinah at my heels, tip-toed out of the house. The eastern sky was flushed, but it was as black as the inside of your hat under the cottage. We crawled around, flashing the light, but could see no Cisco. As she was backing out of the cramped quarters, Dinah knocked over the stack of old dishes she stored there for sand-pile purposes.

"SHHH!" I sounded my war-cry. "You'll wake up Auntie."

A pleasant and slightly bored voice penetrated the floor above me. "If that's all you're worrying about, Auntie's been awake for hours."

I wiggled out onto the terrace, swearing profusely and tearing my nightgown on a nail. "I'm terribly sorry, Alice," I began, "but the cat—"

"I know all about it," my sister said. "I haven't missed a trick since you came barging into my room." Barging, she said, after all my pains! And the cat was still crying somewhere close at hand. I stood up and looked around.

There on the roof, a few feet above my head, was that fool of a Cisco, in the pink of perfect health and bright as a button in the clear, blue, luminous air of early dawn. No wonder his voice had sounded loud and near. He'd been following us around over our heads as we went from room to room. Now that he had our attention, he strolled to the gable, sat down with the first rays of the rising sun bright on his out-thrust chest, and gazed off toward Woods Hole in a detached and snooty manner.

I was mad. Here I'd roused the whole house and wasted all that worry. I said sharply, "You come down off that roof! And don't you look slant-eyed at *me!*" Because that was what he was doing, and I didn't like it. The odd thing was, he couldn't come down. I had to climb up on a window bow and get him. I still bear the scars.

By this time it was five o'clock of what was going to be

a perfectly gorgeous day. So I said, "The heck with it. I'm going swimming and make some coffee. The rest of you go back to sleep." But everyone, even Rufus, was wide awake. We all got up and put in a full day before eight o'clock and time to collect Alice Folsom.

When we drew up on Cannon Street, she came out inquiring, "How'd you sleep, Alice? Do I detect a haggard look?"

"Oh, be quiet!" I said. "How did I know the cat was going to get marooned on the roof?"

Folsom laughed and ignored me. "I suppose you know your own relatives better than I do, Hoke, but in case you hadn't guessed, the whole bunch of them are crazier than Dick's hat-band. Even the cat."

"To-night will be different," I began, but was hooted into silence.

That night was different.

After lunch Rufus and Don Correia asked me if they could sleep out on the beach that night, and I said it was all right with me, if it was all right with Ruth, and if Dinah would be willing to lend Don her sleeping bag. All the ifs worked out, so the boys spent the rest of the day picking out a good place to sleep. They chose a spot midway between their respective homes, and from the preparations they made, you would have thought they were going on safari to the Zambesi. They tried out the sleeping bags—this was at four in the afternoon—and dug little hollows for their hips and shoulders. They found a large, tight tin box and filled it with oranges, cookies, and doughnuts, in case they got hungry during the night; and they buried four bottles of Coke in the sand near their heads, in case they got thirsty. Then they borrowed my portable radio, which will work either on current or on battery, in case they felt the need of light entertainment. At the ungodly hour of eight-thirty, when it was scarcely dark, they went to bed. In due time, the rest of us delivered Alice Folsom to her Aunt Alice's, and I had to listen to more persiflage on the subject of Alice Hoke's sleeping well.

"Now look," I said patiently. "Why shouldn't she sleep well? The dog stays out. The cat won't try that trick again. Rufus is put away for the night, and—"

"And she didn't get much sleep last night, so she ought to pass out cold," Alice Folsom finished for me. "I trust so. Good night."

Before we went to bed at about ten-thirty, my sister and I strolled over to inspect the boys. They were dead to the world, worn out, no doubt, by their labors at setting up camp. The moonlight shone on their unconscious faces, and they looked like a couple of not-so-little angels.

At midnight on the dot I was awakened from the sleep commonly accredited to the just by the banging of the kitchen screen, a slight scuffle, and a lot of giggling. Talk about girls giggling! Have you ever listened to two adolescent boys? "What's going on out there?" I demanded.

"Shhh!" Rufus said with all the tonal delicacy of a locomotive blowing off steam. "I forgot my flashlight, and we might need it." I thought that the less arguing I did, the sooner they'd get out of there and allow peace to reign, so I just snorted. They found the light and retired.

At one o'clock there was more giggling, and a stern command of "Shut *up,* Don. You'll wake up my aunt." It seemed that now they were thirsty and ready to drink the Coke, but had forgotten the bottle opener.

At two o'clock the refrigerator door slammed, and I got up like an avenging Fury and sailed into the kitchen. Gee, they were sorry, but the door got away from them.

"What are you doing in the refrigerator anyhow?" I wanted to know, putting all the venom I could into what had to be a whisper on account of Tired Auntie. Well, it was like this. They'd eaten up all their emergency rations and were still hungry. I gave them a box of fig newtons and promised them that if they set foot in that cottage again that night, I would flay them alive.

They retired somewhat subdued, and a voice from the bed-room said, "Since you're up anyhow, Louise, would you hand me a cigarette and an ash-tray?"

"Honest, Alice, I'm sorry. Those darn brats—"

"Oh, that's all right. This comes under the heading of Seeing Life, I guess. The Seamy Side." My sister giggled to herself. "It reminds me of that time when we were kids, do you remember? When—" I got her cigarette and one for myself, and we smoked and reminisced for fifteen minutes. Then I went back to bed and to sleep.

At four o'clock the door of the car, parked out by the road and right outside my sister's window, slammed and the horn screamed. I leaped out of bed and rushed outside in my nightclothes. I'd left the key in the car, as usual, and this was plainly a case of car theft. I could see dark figures moving around inside it, against the silver sheen of Pine Island Pond, so I picked up a piece of drift-wood and strode over, mad enough not to be scared.

"Gee, Ma," came Rufus' voice, and I was glad to observe that he had the sense and grace to sound a little intimidated, "we didn't mean to blow the horn. I leaned on it by accident."

"What in the name of Hannah are you doing in there anyhow?" I snarled, excusably—I think—irritated. "Honest to goodness, I'm going to kill you kids."

"Well, gosh, we couldn't sleep because the sleeping bags got full of sand from us crawling in and out of them, and you told us not to come in the house, so we thought we'd spend the rest of the night in the car."

"*What* rest of the night?" I asked bitterly. I stomped back into the house, so blind with rage that I fell over the foot-tub full of water that we kept on the back porch for the rinsing of feet before entering, to prevent any more sand than necessary being tracked in for me to sweep up. It fell with a ringing clang to the bricks of the terrace below, and my sister started laughing. "Crazier than Dick's hat-band is right," she remarked.

But why go on? The next night was the night Dinah wanted to sleep on the beach. "—because if the boys can, why can't I, gee whiz? Gee, Ma, I was good and let Don take my sleeping bag, and I don't see why I can't— Gee, what's the use of *having* a sleeping bag if you never get to use it?"

"All *right!*" I said finally. I was stuck and I knew it. Only nine, she certainly couldn't sleep out there alone, and I knew who'd have to sleep out with her. "But once we get into bed, we're not going to get out for *any* reason. For any reason *whatsoever!* Understand?"

She understood.

Everyone, for some strange reason, seemed very willing to go to bed early that night. It was a lovely night for sleeping out, and as soon as we had delivered Alice Folsom to her aunt's house, Dinah and I crawled into our sleeping bags. We lay there looking at the stars and listening to the quiet wash of the little breakers on the shore. The air was soft and warm, and our beds on the sand surprisingly comfortable. We could hear the voices of the people in neighboring cottages murmuring along, and occasionally the shuffle of pebbles as strollers, lured outside by the beauty of the night, walked along below the high-tide mark, talking softly. Cleveland Ledge Light flashed on-off-on-off, paced and steady as the beating of a great, quiet heart. An excursion boat, blazing like a carnival, passed along the channel of the Canal, three miles out. The sound of a dog barking over on Point Connett drifted through the still air, faraway and faint and lacking in urgency.

"Good-night, dear," I said. "Now let's go to sleep fast."

Dinah's voice came back drowsily. "'Sleep already, Ma. 'Night."

Just as my weighted lids were about to close for keeps, a dark shape blanked out the stars, and I was aware of a form bending over me. "Oh, it's you," said the voice of the young woman down-along the point. "What are you doing out here?" I explained, and she said, "I'm at loose ends. Joe left for Cincinnati this morning, and I miss him. The children are in bed, the maid is reading a True Story Magazine, and I'm out looking for trouble to get into."

"Sit down," I invited, and she collapsed with the cross-legged grace of the young and limber. "If you've got a cigarette on you, light me one too, and let's talk of cabbages and kings."

She laughed, produced a cigarette from the pocket of her shorts, and said, "Do you love *Alice*—"—Ooh, that word!—"too?"

"'I've been thinking of a plan to dye one's whiskers

green, and then to use so large a fan that they could not be seen,' " I quoted.

" 'So now, whene'er I chance to put my fingers into glue, or madly squeeze a right-hand foot into a left-hand shoe,' " she countered, and we both chuckled. Then, suddenly serious, she said, "It's funny how I miss Joe."

"Well, I don't know," I objected, being an Older, More Experienced, and Wiser Woman. "If you don't miss your husband when he's away, it's time you found another one."

"Yes, but you see, it's different with us. Ours was a war marriage and we had a terrible time when he came back from overseas. I hadn't seen him in four years—I'd been married less than a week when he left—and—" It was a really interesting story. Before it was done, we'd smoked a whole pack of cigarettes and it was almost two in the morning. She rose and stretched and said, "Well, now that you know the story of my life, I guess I'll go to bed. Thanks a lot for listening, and good night." She padded off down the dark and silent beach, and I went to sleep.

At five-thirty in the morning I was awakened by a presence. I opened my eyes to find a strange man bending over me in the level rays of the rising sun. "Well! You *did* stay out all night. My wife and I saw you and the little girl laying out the sleeping bags, and we made a bet you'd be in your own beds by midnight." He backed away to a distance of about fifteen feet, and to my horror and chagrin, took a picture of us lying there, all blowsey and disheveled. As soon as he had taken himself off, I unzipped myself from the sleeping bag and went into the house to make coffee, preparatory to going swimming. My sister was awake.

"Well," I said brightly, "at last we can confound Folsom. Or at least I hope you had a good night's sleep?"

"Madame DuBarry," she said. "Or was it Madame Pompadour who held conversations in her boudoir at all hours? I missed some of it. What was that chapter about going to a domestic relations expert? I *wish* you'd talk either louder or softer. It's infuriating to be able to hear just enough to know what it's all about, but not enough really to follow the thread."

CHAPTER NINE

The Excursion

AFTER Alice Folsom went home, I and mine were inspired by my sister into a great spurt of sudden activity. It started with the shell collection, so-called. In our sloppy and unscientific way, we'd simply been picking up shells as we happened upon them, and dropping them into an A&P shopping bag hung on a door-knob. We didn't really know why. The magpie instinct, perhaps. We just liked sea shells, so various and intricate and delicate in structure and, to us, new. My sister, who has an orderly mind and a cool curiosity about almost everything, was not content with this system. She wanted to know the names of the things, and she pointed out to me, quite rightly, that I was wasting an opportunity for the children's education. I agreed, but this meant buying a book. Ruth Correia told me that there was a good bookstore in New Bedford. So off with bathing suits, on with our cotton dresses and canvas hats—our version of Dressing Up For The City—and heigh-ho for New Bedford.

That is a dilly of a city in which to drive. All the streets are narrow and over-crowded and up-hill or down-dale, and many of them are one-way. That would be all right, except that in the middle of a block—or so it seemed to my fevered mind—they change their minds, and you discover that you are proceeding in the wrong direction on a one-way street, a disconcerting experience.

While I was coping with such a situation by driving straight along, eyes front, and getting my tongue limbered to say, "I'm *so* sorry, Officer! I'm a stranger here and I'm afraid I didn't see the traffic sign," my sister exclaimed, "This is where they have that whaling museum. It's supposed to be the best in the world. The kids ought to see it, and I'd love to." She'd recently written a book, "Amazing Animals," among them whales, and I suppose she wanted to check on herself.

We found the bookstore with only moderate difficulty and bought a book called "A Field Guide to the Shells of Our Atlantic and Gulf Coasts," by Percy A. Morris, published by Houghton Mifflin Co. It is a marvelous book, with hundreds of illustrations and so lucid a text that even we soon learned to distinguish between True and False Angel Wings, both Pelecypods, but the one Genus Petricola and the other Genus Barnea. No that you are interested. I merely want to show off my erudition.

I asked the lady in charge where we'd find the Whaling Museum, and she said go right back down Union Street and turn left up Johnny Cake Hill. Then she looked at us narrowly. "You're summer people, aren't you?"

There was no object in denying it, so we admitted the gentle impeachment.

"Nothing to be ashamed of at all," she reassured us broad-mindedly. "I was only going to say, if you're new to these parts, you might enjoy a trip to Cuttyhunk. The boat leaves at a little after ten every morning, from Pier Three." She chuckled pleasantly. "I don't own stock in the company. I just like to have folks have a good time."

That was an idea. See what you get into by buying a book? We thanked her and set out for Johnny Cake Hill and the Whaling Museum.

Museums in general fail to strike a spark in my breast. Ordinarily I darken their doors only to find out something I think I have to know. But this museum is different. It has some bearing on life. It's a wonderful place. We stayed there four hours, and it wasn't anywhere nearly long enough. The most dramatic exhibit is the largest ship model in the world, a half-size replica of the whaling bark *Lagoda.* It's big enough so that you can walk all over it, even below deck. It's complete in every detail and, to put it mildly, very interesting.

My sister asked the guard to point out to Dinah the bones of the vestigial legs of the skeleton of the whale, and he was so moved that he almost wept on her shoulder from joy. He took right over and gave us a personally conducted tour and lecture. That's what it means to have an intelligent sister. Apparently not everyone knows that whales have legs. It pays off. Thanks to Alice's being a Really Informed Woman, we learned a great deal.

I'm not going to bore you with a catalogue of the contents of the Old Dartmouth Historical Society and Whaling Museum. If you're ever around New Bedford, go and see for yourself, *not* skipping the exhibit of scrimshaw or the idle-work common seamen did on their own time, going 'round the Horn, to save them from insanity. Look at the ivory carvings on children's sleds— Oh heck! I said I wouldn't bore you. But may I tell you about the thing I loved best? It was a doll house. This museum contains other things than the appurtenances of whaling; it's also an historical museum. It has a whole room devoted to old dolls and doll houses.

My particular doll house was tall, taller than I, and inhabited by a family of exquisite five-inch china dolls, who seemed to be living a most peculiar family life. In the attic, all by herself, was an old witch-woman at a spinning wheel. On the floor below, in the best bed-room, was a lady of interesting age, either arising or retiring. I couldn't tell which. She was half-way into or out of bed, wearing a sheer, long-sleeved, throat-high, blue-ribboned night-gown. Maybe she was an interesting invalid, in a decline from a broken heart or what used to be known as The Vapors. What threw me off my stride was the scene in the front parlor.

There, there was a young lady seated on a sofa, looking maidenly, receiving a proposal from an impassioned young man on his knees before her. She had on a wide-brimmed, rough-straw hat with a flower wreath, what I would call a garden-party hat. But would you wear one of those in the evening, when your aunt might be going to bed? No. But would you be receiving a proposal at the time in the morning that your aunt might be getting up? I can speak only from my own experience, and in my experience of many years, it's hard to get a civil word out of a man before noon, let alone an honest proposal.

In the living-room, across the hall, was a mature woman in a very apprehensive attitude. She was cowering in her wing-chair and looking fearfully at a man who, I suppose, was her husband, an elegant gent with side-burns and a mustache. His face was contorted with rage, he was striking a pose with gestures, and under his foot was the cause of his tantrum, a miniature newspaper slightly larger than an air-mail stamp. By pressing our noses on the glass protecting the exhibit and straining our eyes, we could just make out the name of the paper. It was the old *Boston Evening Transcript.*

Alice and I had been brought up on the *Transcript,* and we couldn't imagine what that organ of conservatism could possibly have printed to drive anyone into such a fury. We decided that either he had a bad case of dyspepsia, or else he was a blackguard to start with. The cellar wasn't shown. We hated to think what might be down there. Probably a drooling idiot in manacles. Speculation kept us well occupied for hours. All right, all right. We have trivial minds. But we also have a lot of fun.

We decided that we'd go to Cuttyhunk on the next fine day, which turned out to be two days later. We set out from Angelica before nine. Anyone else could make the boat in half an hour, probably, but the way I drive and the way I get lost, we thought we should allow a good generous hour.

The minute we crossed the bridge into New Bedford, we got lost, naturally. I had just drawn up to the curb to inquire of a pedestrian, when a police prowl car came to a halt beside me. Of course my first thought was that I was again going east on a west-bound street; but the officer simply said mildly, "What's the matter? Lost?" Apparently it is no new experience in the lives of the New Bedford cops to run across lost motorists roaming their streets, a fact which made me feel a little better. He set us right, and we had to inquire only about three times more before actually arriving at Pier Three.

The Cuttyhunk boat is the *Alert,* a broad-beamed, sturdy, half-cabin job with a covered after-deck. I tried to pay the man who seemed to be in charge as we boarded, but he told me no, he liked to catch passengers out in the middle, where they couldn't escape. Then he went back to supervising the loading of the freight. We sat down on benches and watched him, and I immediately began to feel at home. This was just like being on Larry's boat, the *Al-Lar,* at Middle Dam, where everything to go up the lakes is dumped in the center of the deck: crates of vegetables, guests' expensive luggage, live hens in boxes, the U.S. Mail, sides of beef, clothes back from the dry-cleaner, and heaven knows what-else in a mounting pile. When I could stand it no longer, I asked, "Don't they grow *anything* on the island?" This was after several ten gallon milk cans and the third crate of green vegetables had been added to the heap.

"Nope. Not to mention. Few heads of lettuce in backyards, maybe. But not much else. You'll see when you get there."

By this time about twenty-five people were aboard, the freight was all secure, and it was time to cast off. After a certain amount of whistle-tooting, we backed out of the slip, turned fussily, and were on our way.

The first thing that Dinah wanted to know, pointing at the enormous sign on top of a water-front factory, was what that word was. I didn't know. It looked like it ought to make sense, but there was something vaguely wrong with it. I didn't know any word YAWAHTAH in English; so I told her that it was doubtless an Indian word.

My sister was studying it with an air of concentration. "Why, no, it isn't either," she said. "It's the back view of HATHAWAY's sign. You know. The baker." And so it was. That is the kind of mind my sister has. She gets to the bottom of things, rather than accept the first facile explanation available. But I think there was some excuse for me. Who'd ever expect a word as long as that to be readable in mirror writing? Most words have one letter at least that looks cock-eyed from the rear, like B or E or N.

By the time we had settled that one, we were out of the harbor and going down the bay. On the right—I suppose that, since this is the tale of the Riches' Day At Sea, I should say starboard—was the mainland, and on the left (port) were the Elizabeth Islands. It was a perfectly beautiful day for a sail, warm, calm, and slightly hazy, so that the land by which we were chugging had a faint, dreamlike quality. We had field glasses with us, and for a while amused ourselves by looking at the shores we were passing. But finally we drew away from the mainland and the islands presented much the same faces: uninhabited dunes and heaths, broken occasionally by a farm house or a fisherman's shack; so we turned our attention to the boat and the people on it. Most of them were just trippers like ourselves and lacking in interest, but there were a few that needed thinking about.

First there was the man in dungarees, dirty white sneakers, a blue chambray shirt, and a base-ball cap. He looked like a member of the crew, except that he was doing nothing except sit and read a book, not even raising his eyes when other craft passed by and all the rest of us were falling over-board in an effort to see and identify them.

My sister and I have an idiosyncrasy in common. We just can't endure seeing anyone reading without learning what. So we took turns strolling past him until we finally spied out that the book he was so absorbed in was something called "You and Your Psychiatrist."

"I don't think he really needs that," my sister muttered. "He seems very well-adjusted and calm. Look, there's a specimen who acts much more emotionally unstable."

The man in question was a nice-looking gentleman in a Pendleton plaid shirt, quite obviously "summer-people." You could tell by his Cordovans. He seemed to have something on his mind. He'd sit awhile, hands loosely clasped between his knees, staring broodingly out at the sea. Then he'd jump up and pace around. Pretty soon it became clear that his pacings were taking him nearer and nearer to the pile of freight, each round he made. At last he stopped fooling and started rustling luggage and chicken crates until he unearthed a large duffle-bag, presumably his own property since he opened it and began removing articles. There were some neck-ties, some shoes, some shirts, a box of chocolates, a new doll in cellophane, and a pair of corduroys with something rolled up in them. Looking about a little furtively, he unrolled the object and thrust it into the bosom of his shirt. It was a fifth of Scotch whiskey.

My sister heaved a sigh of relief. "There! That's taken care of! Now everything will be dandy," she said, as our man went sloping off toward the men's room. "Or do you think we still ought to ask our quiet friend to lend our restless friend his book? Maybe we could save a lost week-end."

"Oh, I don't know," I told her. "I'd like nothing better,

considering the business I'm in, than to rely absolutely on the complete power of the written word. But I have a feeling that it would take more than just reading a book to calm that one down." At this point That One came back from his hide-out, looking much better and more composed, and returned his bottle to his duffle-bag. Alice and I decided against any spot of missionary work for the moment. He was doing all right on his own.

Anyhow, two things were happening simultaneously that demanded our attention. Dinah came back from a reconnaissance, during which she had penetrated the fastnesses of the pilot-house, to report that the man had a great big turtle in there with him; and the *Alert,* for no reason that we could see, since we were out in the middle of the bay, miles from any land, was coming to a full stop. We postponed the turtle investigation until later, and practically hung by our toes over the rail to see what was going on.

A small fishing smack, heretofore hidden from us by the cabin, was drawing alongside. A man, presumably the captain, was standing at the prow with a megaphone in his hand. As soon as he was within hollering distance, he hollered. "Ahoy, *Alert!* When you get in, will you tell the Coast Guard that Benjie's aground on the Banks and needs help gettin' off? We got it over the ship-to-shore, but he can't raise the Coast Guard. He ain't in any danger. He jest wants to git home. His catch is spoilin' on him, an' besides, his wife is expectin' him."

The man that had been so off-hand about making us pay our fare shouted back that sure, he'd let the Coast Guard know, and how did Benjie get himself into such a fix, calm weather like this? The reply was lost as the boats drew apart. This exchange put me right back into the sticks of Maine, where, when the communication systems break down, as they do frequently, you can always depend on the grapevine to get your message through. The *Alert* picked up sea-way, Alice and I went to view the rumored turtle, and Rufus came tearing along from the bow, where he had been fraternizing with the deck-hands, to announce that Cuttyhunk was in sight. Dinah went in search of a drink of water, and Alice and I settled down with the field glasses to study the approach.

Cuttyhunk was there all right in the distance, but there was an unexplained island off the starboard bow. Alice raked it with the glasses and said to me, "Boy! That's where I'm going to retire to in my old age. Take a look. Those buildings aren't inhabited, are they? Wouldn't it be a *wonderful* place—?"

I took the glasses and stared through them at the small island in question. There was what we call in Maine a nice set of buildings: a weather-beaten salt-box house, a large barn, a corral, a boathouse,—all in a state of moderate disrepair—and a small harbor, protected by a rock jetty. There was nothing else at all that we could see on that island except rocks, grass, scrub trees, and a ridge rising in back of the house just where it would serve as shelter from the gales of winter. We couldn't see a sign of animal life anywhere.

"Wow," I said, my pulse quickening, "wouldn't I love to own that one." I've always wanted to own an island, and there is nothing in the world I love better than playing around with an old, broken-down house, trying to make something out of it. I've had just enough of it at Forest Lodge to whet my appetite. I marked that island down on my mental list of things to be looked into at a future date.

We were now entering the channel to the harbor of Cuttyhunk, and there was too much going on for Alice and me to brood longer on desert islands. Clouds of gulls were rising to wheel and scream around us. I know gulls are dirty to have around in any numbers, but they are beautiful to look at in the air, handling themselves so expertly on the currents, and their plaintive mewing has a wild and exciting quality. I rounded up the kids, preparatory to debarking, and we watched the gulls, and the shore sliding by so near you could spit on it, and finally the people meeting the boat. They were so interesting that we almost forgot to get off ourselves.

First of all, our boy with the bottle vaulted off, to be met and embraced by a pretty woman who was obviously his wife. I could tell by the way she kissed him, smelled his breath, and put a half-admonitory, half-affectionate hand against his cheek. There was a flock of small, sun-bleached children, equally obviously his own, milling about. He kissed them all around and went off with them in a station wagon. My sister and I decided that we didn't have to worry about him. He was in good, ballasting hands.

Then our boy with the book went ashore with great dignity to the perfunctory kiss of a gray-haired woman in a seersucker dress and sensible shoes, who could be nothing other than a professor's wife. Hmmm. So he was a professor, probably of psychology. We apologized silently for mistaking him for a roustabout; but on mature reflection I don't think we should have. Could he have read our minds, he should have been flattered.

Eventually we found ourselves in a lunchroom called

the Sea Breeze. I was all for looking for a tonier eating establishment, but my off-spring were saying, "Gee, Ma, I'm *dying*. Gee whiz, when do we eat? Jeepers, Ma, we're *hongry!*" They were also managing, in spite of their ebony tans, high color, and visible states of robust health, to look like under-nourished, pallid, hollow-eyed refugees. It's a trick that they can pull at a moment's notice, and I wish that I possessed the secret of it. It would come in handy at times, like when I might like to pose as a pitiful widow, with two starving children to support, badly in need of help. The occasion hasn't arisen yet, but you never can tell.

However, that is all beside the point. To get on, I said to my sister, "Do you mind terribly? If we don't feed these animals immediately, we'll have no peace at all. And if there is a local representative of the SPCC, she'll slam me into the hoose-gow sure as shooting as a cruel parent, if she gets an eyeful and earful of this."

My sister said good-naturedly that she didn't mind at all. And that is how we landed in the Sea Breeze, and I'm glad that we did. The food was good, and the atmosphere informal. We enjoyed it.

But we gained more than that. It seemed that it was the place where the workingman ate, and pretty soon the crew of the *Alert* came drifting in. In the course of the morning they and we had become old friends, so we felt free to ask questions as we all leaned in a matey manner on the counter and sipped our coffee. First off the pickle boat, I wanted to know about that island off to the north, the one with the abandoned buildings on it.

The counterman, free from duty for a minute, joined the circle. "Why, that's Penikese. You must have heard. The old leper colony. When I was a kid, they had a shoal of lepers over there, but after a while they shipped them out to Carville, Louisiana. The government took over and started raising rabbits, but I don't know what happened. It petered out somehow. Guess there wasn't enough feed for them. Them dunes are pretty bleak, and you'd be surprised at how much grass a couple-thousand rabbits can eat. So now it's a bird sanctuary, which means the gulls nest on it and maybe a sandpiper or two." I didn't have to have teeter-ass explained to me. We have them on the inland waters of Maine. They are sandpipers. The inelegant but descriptive colloquialism is derived from the way their little rear ends bob up and down as they skitter along the shore.

"But what about the buildings?" I asked. "Aren't they used at all?"

"Oh, yeah. Couple of times a year the game warden camps out there over night, maybe to count the gulls, maybe for the heck of it. Nobody else goes near. Place has got a bad name, account of them lepers. Too bad. They never did no one no harm."

A crewman spoke up. "Lot of nonsense about leprosy. It ain't all that catchin'. I don't claim to know the ins and outs of it, but I'll tell you this, ma'am. If 'twas as catchin' as some folks an' the New Testament think, we'd have all had it years ago, livin' an' born an' bred on this island, like us all were, so near to Penikese. Nope. If I had the cash, know what I'd do? I'd try to buy that island or take out squatters' rights on it, old leper colony or no old leper colony. Maybe its reputation would keep my creditors off my neck." He wiped his lips on a paper napkin and paid for his lunch. "I'd move the wife and kids over there. A man could have a good life on Penikese, if he didn't mind the lonesomeness. Some folks, like me, like lonesomeness, like not bein' crowded in on. Them poor lepers," he said. "I get to thinkin' about them nights. Some of them liked it over on Penikese. I used to talk to them, kid-fashion, out ground-fishin' for scup in a dory. Then they got moved to Louisiana, without havin' an aye-yes-or-no in the matter. Me, I never been to Louisiana, an' I got no hankerin' to go. Don't think I'd like it. Too green an' hot. It's an awful thing, ma'am, to be shoved around when it ain't your fault."

I thought that over, and found that there was nothing I could add. He'd said it all. So, as he left the lunchroom, I asked the proprietor how best we could put in our two hours before sailing time. He said that if he were we, he'd climb up to the look-out tower, on the highest point of the island, right thataway, ma'am. From there we could get a general notion of the lay-out.

So we climbed up narrow pathways, between hedges of wild roses, to the tower, and I was appalled to see by what a precarious finger-nail grip the human race maintained possession of this scrap of land. The little village huddled below us under the lea of the hill, which was really only a large dune. The greater part of the island, to the southwest, was uninhabited moor, marked at the further extreme by the bright, unwinking eye of Gosnold Pond. On an islet in the pond is an old fortification, the top of which we could just see. It was built in 1602 by Gosnold, the discoverer of the island, as a protection against the Indians, and I wish we'd had time to go down and inspect it. We hadn't, so we sat on the parched grass and looked at it, happy in the knowledge that it dated eighteen years before the Pilgrims and Plymouth Rock; and we

On an islet in the pond is an old fortification. We looked at it, happy in the knowledge that it dated eighteen years before the Pilgrims and Plymouth Rock.

watched the great combers roll in from Spain and dash themselves to death on the seaward side. Alice and I had just been reading Rachel Carson's wonderful book, "The Sea Around Us," and maybe that fired our imaginations. While the kids chased butterflies, we talked about the ocean, and its great power and presence.

A friend of mine once asked what in the world my sister and I found as subjects of conversation that we could yak-yak-yak for hours on end. Well, now you know. We can yak about almost anything. We just love the sounds of our own voices.

Reluctantly we sauntered down-dune to the harbor and the *Alert,* which was nowhere near ready to sail. So we took off our shoes and went wading, not a very dignified public occupation for grown women, but pleasant. The channel into the harbor of Cuttyhunk is so narrow that if you wade out to your knees, you practically have your chin in the scuppers of in-coming vessels. There were yachts from all over the western hemisphere going in and out, and I was pretty much impressed.

I was especially impressed by an eighty-foot, as nearly as I could estimate from my vantage point, mahogany job prowling up the channel to anchorage. On the bridge were three officers in full uniform, with presses in their pants that would cut your arm off at the wrist, if you were so careless as to lay a gentle hand on a knee in the course of conversation. There was the captain, brass to the elbow, studying the channel through binoculars and giving quiet orders like "Port your helm." There was a mate, stripes half-way to the elbow, intent on the business of steering and saying, "Aye-aye, sir; port helm." There was a second mate, no stripes. (Maybe he was only the janitor or whatever the sea-going equivalent is, dressed up for the occasion.) He was standing on the steps, (Companionway? I must consult some of my nautical friends about these terms.), saying nothing, but alert for an emergency. Brother, were they bringing that boat into port with great style. I *love* a stylish performance and people who know what they are doing and go ahead and do it without fuss.

On the after-deck under an awning were the owners, lounging in deck chairs, sipping high-balls, and paying no attention. They were used, apparently, to coming into port with dash. They were fat and elderly.

I said to my sister, "That's for me. That is how I would like to live, if I could afford it."

She gave me a look of horror over her bunched-up skirt that she was trying to keep dry. "Why, Sarah Louise Dickinson, you would not! With your claustrophobia? You'd hate being cooped up on a boat. Anyhow, land is the stuff to own. Land lasts forever. Come a hurricane, where's your boat and your investment?"

I meekly admitted that she was right, and we launched into a discussion about property-ownership, with the sea lapping about our knees, while the kids skimmed flat stones and the *Alert* got itself together to sail.

When we arrived back at Angelica, we discovered that that was the day we should have stayed at home. Ruth Correia came over to inform us that they'd needed Rufus badly while we were away. Don and Mrs. Flodin's young daughter had lost an oar out in the middle of the bay, and were being carried to sea when sighted.

"Of course," said Ruth, "this would be the day every man on the beach was away, and you know how much I know about starting an outboard motor. Nothing. We were screaming around for Rufus, and then Mrs. Thompson told us he'd gone to Cuttyhunk. Don't go away again for the day. We can't spare Rufus that long."

I laughed and Rufus was so flattered that he expanded through the chest two full sizes. "How did you get the kids in?" I asked.

"Oh, I finally managed to get the kicker started. It's funny what you find you can do, if your young-ones are in danger."

And ain't that the truth.

My sister flopped into a chair. "I'm not a mother, but one thing is becoming very clear to me. If you belong to that sorority, you never have a dull moment."

She could certainly say that again!

CHAPTER TEN

Summer's End

THAT shell collection was responsible for more than a trip to the Whaling Museum and Cuttyhunk. In the avid search for more and different and better shells, the children naturally ran across various live marine creatures, and an aquarium was inevitable. I thought this would be a simple device to keep my young out of trouble and occupied, so I said they could have the foot-tub off the porch—the one in which we rinsed sand from our feet—for their project. For it I substituted the inadequate hand basin out of the kitchen sink, thereby exposing Alice Folsom, down to spend a day, to shock. She had occasion to de-sand before entering the kitchen, and for a horrible moment there she thought her feet had grown all that much in the past two weeks, and began screaming like a banshee about her metabolism.

There is more to having an amateur aquarium than would appear on the surface. My first innocent idea was that we'd just fill the tub with sea water and then let it alone, except for dumping in new specimens as we found them. But my sister was sure that this would not do at all. We should have suitable surroundings for our pets, like sand and rocks and various types of sea-weed, and we should change the water every day. We should keep the so-called aquarium in the shade, since the sun heated the small amount of water possible in the pan, and consequently all our captives would soon die. She was undoubtedly right, so we put the thing in a corner of the terrace by the front steps, sacrificing a few of my nasturtiums to make room; and I added, "Have you changed the aquarium water?" to my daily Hounding List, which already carried such items as "Have you fed the dog?", "Have you swept the terrace, Dinah?", "Have you buried the garbage, Rufus?", "Have you hung up your wet bathing suits?", "Have you put out the milk bottles?", and so on, almost *ad infinitum.*

Note: Like all parents, I know it would be much easier and take less time to do all these things myself; but we have to have a little discipline and recognition of responsibility once in a while, don't we?

We collected some minnows, barnacles, periwinkles, snails, and assorted small bivalves, and we had a very good time watching them. Dinah had one scallop about as large as your little fingernail that was especially fascinating. She named it Hoppsie-Fleasie, because it hopped like a flea. I didn't know that scallops, and I guess most bivalves, have a long foot that they usually keep folded into their shells. But when they want to go somewhere in a hurry, they thrust it out and vault along on it. Boy, they can travel! They also, when feeding—or maybe only to change the water inside their homes—clap their shells together furiously. There was a great deal of activity in that foot-tub, if you had the patience to sit down quietly and watch. We spent a lot of time leaning over it breathlessly. That's where some of my summer went, so that I didn't finish my book.

"We ought to have a couple of star-fish," my sister said thoughtfully one day.

"There aren't any around here," I told her confidently. Alice Folsom's Uncle Billy Johnson had told me so. She looked regretful.

But the next day she and the children went for a long walk around the further, uninhabited, extreme end of Angelica, and came back with bunches of sea lavender, a rusty coffee can, and airs of triumph.

"I thought you said there weren't any star-fish around here," Rufus crowed, and showed me the contents of the can, three star-fish.

"We could have got a lot more," Dinah informed me loftily, her eyes snapping. "But Auntie said the tub wasn't big enough for more than three. They'd starve to death. We kept this one because it was the biggest, and this one because it was a 'specially good shape, and this one—"

As she paused, I looked at This One. It was the darndest thing I ever saw. If it had had all its rays, it would have been slightly larger than a fifty cent piece; but it had only two. Where the other three should have been there were just little buds. It looked neither handsome nor healthy to me. "Just why *did* you keep this one?"

My sister lighted a cigarette. "Well, I'll tell you. I'm sure I read somewhere that if a star-fish lost a ray through an accident, it would grow another. I just wanted to see if it could possibly grow three more. It won't do any harm to put him in the tank and see."

After the advent of the star-fish, the aquarium took up even more of our time. In fact, I might almost go so far as to say that it monopolized our time. We didn't know anything about star-fish, and of course they weren't listed in our shell book. So we had to fly blind, using what poor wits we possessed. To start with, we didn't know what they ate, but decided—the Lord knows why, unless it was because we'd been reading Rachel Carson and remembered a lot of "Kon-tiki"—that they probably ate plankton. We were uncertain of the amount of plankton in one small foot-tubful of water, but suspected that it would be insufficient for the needs of three star-fish, one of them a two-legged-growing boy, so to speak. So at least once a day we took them down to the ocean and turned them loose, riding herd on them while they had, we hoped, a good square meal. They took a lot of herd-riding. Those things can move fast, if they want to, and have a sly habit of hiding themselves by smart use of their protective coloring, if you turn your back for a second.

Then we weren't sure whether the oxygen supply was enough for them, so we had to change the water frequently. They had a trick of going to the surface and turning upside down, exposing their orange linings and hundreds of what we thought were feelers, and sort of gasping for air. When they did this, we'd rush with a pail of new sea water, like nurses with oxygen tanks or Seppala with the serum for Nome. After they'd been revived by this treatment, they had a nasty way of chasing Hoppsie and the other small denizens of the tank around, putting them into a dither and exhausting the poor little things both nervously and physically. So we'd have to remove Hoppsie *et al* to a smaller pan temporarily for a rest cure.

I'm not fooling, we were pretty busy there for a spell, day *and* night.

Mrs. Thompson, next door, said to me one morning, "Was that boy of yours going swimming in the middle of the night? I was up with my grand-daughter; she wasn't feeling so good. Must have been around two o'clock. I looked out and saw Rufus running down to the water. Funny time to go swimming, I thought to myself. Not safe, this time of night and no one around."

"Oh, no," I said. "He was just changing the aquarium water."

She looked at me oddly. "Well, seems to me you folks make an awful lot of trouble for yourselves; but I suppose you know what you're doing."

The first part of her surmise was absolutely correct, but the second was certainly open to question. We found that out the day that the largest star-fish lost a ray. There he was, undulating around with four legs, his amputated member loose on the bottom. We made up our minds that it was time to consult an expert. Since he was going to die anyhow, we removed him and his lost ray from the tub and threw them into the ocean. Then we high-tailed it for the library and borrowed a book called "The Sea Beach at Ebb Tide," or something like that.

What we found out about star-fish! We'd had *everything* wrong. They are practically indestructible, no matter what you do to them, short of pitching them out into the middle of the Sahara. They do not eat plankton. They eat shell-fish, and are so destructive of oyster-beds that oystermen conduct an intensive and expensive war against them. What we thought were feelers are suction cups, and they can open an oyster with them, folding themselves around it and applying the old suction. It may take hours, but they always win in the end. Then they devour the soft flesh within. If you have ever tried to open an oyster with the same idea in mind, you know it's no cinch. Furthermore, a star-fish can at will cast off one of its rays, and he does it when in danger, when angry, or when just plain bored, as was probably the case with ours. No harm at all is done. He grows another and the abandoned part parlays itself into a new star-fish. In fact, oyster-men used to chop them up and throw the pieces over-board, until they discovered that they were simply increasing the population by leaps and bounds. Now they take them ashore and dump them at a good safe distance inland.

We looked at each other sadly, and then went and looked at the aquarium, where Baby was busily developing his three new rays. Oh, well, we hadn't completely wasted our time. Employing our usual method, The Hard Way, we'd learned something.

As we were brooding over this turn of Fate, George Gardner, with his young daughters Ruth and Mary, came driving along the point to see if Rufus and Dinah wanted to go to the village to the band concert with them. It seems that the band concerts and the outdoor square dances are a weekly feature of the summer social life of Mattapoisett.

Dinah, always one for keeping her neck in, wanted to know what one did at a band concert. She'd never been to one, and she wasn't going to get out on any limb where she'd have to sing a solo or something. On being assured that you listened to the band play (my version) and bought ice-cream cones and played tag with all the other kids (Ruth's and Mary's version), she was very eager indeed to go. I re-tied her hair-ribbons, gave her a quarter, and instructed her to be a good girl and mind Dr. Gardner; and off they went. Alice and I settled down to a nice quiet evening with good books, our first since Poor Tired Auntie had arrived. But after about fifteen minutes of peace, I got to worrying.

"Gee, I hope the kids behave themselves. It seems to me that George is undertaking quite a lot, poor guy. He's supposed to be on his vacation, after all."

Alice looked up from her book. "Isn't he the Director of some child guidance foundation and a pretty well-known child psychiatrist? I don't think I'd worry much about him. His business is handling kids. Stop stewing."

She went back to her book and I went back to stewing, only in silence now. After all, much as I love my children, I am not blind to the fact that they can act *awful,* especially when they get excited.

At a little after ten, we heard a car door slam out back, and cries of "Good-night! We had a wonderful time, thank you," and the kids came bursting into the house, radiating *joie de vivre.*

"Marty and Sheila went too," they exclaimed, "and gee, did we ever have fun!" I guess from all accounts they did. They'd had ice-cream, played tag and hide-and-seek, organized teams for spying on people, stalked each other through the crowd, and oh just *everything,* Ma!

"And *what,*" I asked in a voice of horror, "was poor Dr. Gardner doing all this while?" I had visions of him flying apart in all directions, trying to keep track of those six limbs.

"Oh, he was sitting on the Holiday House porch with his feet up," Rufus explained in a tone of sweet reason.

"Heck, he didn't care anything about playing tag. He just told us where we could and couldn't go, and made us all promise to report to him at Headquarters—that was the hotel porch—every half hour. So we did."

Against my better judgment, I looked at my sister. She was gazing carefully at a corner of the ceiling, her eyebrows high, her lips disciplined against a smile. She might just as well have come right out and said, "See? I told you so."

To cover my confusion, I asked, "Was the band good?"

"Band?" For a moment both the young faces were blank. "Oh. Band. Oh, sure, I guess they were all right," Rufus said, and that disposed of the main attraction of the evening. "Hey, I got to get up early to-morrow. Dr. Gardner's coming down, and we're going scup fishing. I got to get the boat ready and find my drop-line and dig some quahogs for bait before he gets here."

George, I thought, is certainly a glutton for punishment. But then I thought again, Will I never learn? Will I never accept the fact that most adults know what they're doing when they get themselves into these things? Why don't you relax, Louise, and let people live their own lives?

Suddenly it was time for Alice to go back to New York, and Labor Day was coming up, and where had the summer gone? From June till September had seemed such a lovely long time, way back then, and now it was almost over, and it didn't seem that we'd been at the beach more than a minute. Of course, we still had September, but the children would be there only over week-ends, and it wouldn't be the same. Sadly we took Auntie, now Brown Healthy Auntie, over to New Bedford and put her on the plane. Then we hurried back to make the most of our diminishing fund of time.

We didn't fritter away any of that fund on further excursions. We stuck to the beach and the old summer-long routine. But the familiar occupations which we had grown to take for granted now assumed their early vividness, only there was an added poignancy to them, the result of knowledge and accumulated experience. Every time we went into E. A. Walsh's, we saw through fresh eyes what a marvelous store it is, and we said to each other, "Remember the day we got stuck here in a thunder-storm?", or, smiling at our early ignorance, "Remember when we had to *ask* where the chocolate bits are kept?" When we lay spread-eagled on the sand, we felt again the sun of June biting into our winter-white shoulders, although now we were the color of old boots and it would have taken a blow-torch to burn any of us. The sea suddenly looked bluer, and the freighters and sailing vessels moving out from the Canal suddenly became again mysterious and romantic barks, bound for who knew what exotic ports, instead of just some traffic passing. Cleveland Ledge Light, which we'd ignored for weeks, we saw again the instant it came on each evening, and we'd sit and look at it, torn by the knowledge that after we had gone and all through the long winter nights, it would still be winking steadfastly. We learned all over again the universal truth that you never really appreciate a thing until you know you are going to lose it. There was nothing we could do to delay the inexorable approach of summer's end.

Labor Day week-end was terrible. We'd been blessed all summer long with beautiful weather, but that week-end made up for it. A cold north-easter blew up Friday night, and continued all day Saturday and all day Sunday. Fog and rain drove in off the ocean, and the sea and the earth and the sky were a uniform dead gray. We built a fire in the Franklin stove and stayed in the house, except for an occasional brisk walk to air our lungs. It was much too cold to go swimming, so we entertained ourselves by making fudge, toasting marshmallows, reading, and assuring each other that (a) it was much worse for the poor people who hadn't been to the beach all summer and had only this week-end in which to enjoy it, and (b) that it would clear off to-morrow, an entirely false premise.

Sunday night at about 9:20 I said, "In ten minutes I want everyone in this house to be in bed. It'll probably clear off to-morrow, and it'll be our last day here before school starts, so we want to get up early and enjoy every minute of it." To my gratified surprise, the children didn't put up any argument, but started brushing teeth and getting undressed.

Dinah was in bed, Rufus had peeled down to his undershorts and was looking for something to eat before completing his disrobing, and I was in the bathroom cold-creaming my face, when a car went racing up the point with Don Correia screaming from the front seat, "Our house is on fire!"

I assumed that he was as bored with the weather as all the rest of us were and was trying to create a little excitement and diversion; so I said disapprovingly to Rufus, "That isn't funny. If I ever hear of your yelling fire just for the heck of it, I'll make you wish you'd never been born. Fire's nothing to kid about." I slapped on some more cold cream in a severe manner.

"Maybe he isn't kidding," Rufus said. "I'm going to

see." He dashed out as he was, in one very inadequate under-garment. As I think I said before, Angelica is an informal place.

In thirty seconds he was back, his eyes bugging. "It *is* on fire, it *is* on fire! Quick, where's the pail? You bring it. I got to go back with our shovel." He was gone before I could blink.

I am terrified of fire, I will admit frankly. I grabbed the pail and ran, with Dinah at my heels in her nightgown. As I rounded the Friedman's cottage on a dead gallop, I saw that this was indeed no joke. All the beams and joists under the cottage around the base of the fire-place chimney were burning, and tongues of flame were licking along the floor boards. Trudy Correia in her night-clothes and a bathrobe was standing shivering and crying on the beach, and Ruth and Mrs. Friedman and her mother, Mrs. Young, were rushing in and out of the kitchen with pans of water. Under the cottage several dark figures were moving frantically around, and it took me a minute in the windy, flame-stained darkness to realize that they were Manny Correia and Mr. Young, trying to shovel sand onto the fire. It is almost impossible to smother a fire over your head with sand, let me tell you. And there was a man I didn't know doing what I didn't know.

Ruth saw me and gasped, "Louise, isn't this terrible? Mr. Campbell's taken Don up to Connett to phone for the Fire Department. If we can only control it until they come—"

I got into the line with my bucket and started yelling for Rufus. I didn't see him anywhere, and he could pass buckets as well as the next one. "He's gone down the point to get more buckets and more help, if there's anyone left.

Most everybody went home to-day, the weather's so bad." Ruth was making more sense than I would have if it had been my house, especially as it was becoming very clear that in spite of all our efforts the fire was getting away from us on the rising gale. And so far we hadn't even heard the alarm sound over in town. Mattapoisett has a volunteer fire department, so a whistle is blown to summon the volunteers, and after that there is a time lapse while they assemble.

It's hard to throw water over your head at a fire to the best advantage, and as I saw a couple of bucketsful half wasted over the shoulders of the stranger doing the strange thing—he seemed to be kneeling in front of the fire, praying—I thought savagely, "If we only had a *hose!*"

"Holy Mackerel!" I exclaimed aloud, and threw my bucket down, cursing myself for thirty-nine kinds of empty-headed fool as I raced back home. I *had* a hose! We used it to hose ourselves off once in a while when we got too salty, and Don and Rufus used it to fill the barrel in which they tested their outboards. It was old and rotten and leaked in seventy places, but water would come out the end of it in a fair stream. It was kept under the porch, and I was almost crying as I tried to tug it loose in the pitch darkness, because of course it got caught on some private cultch—Mainese for assorted junk—the kids had stored there. If only I'd used my pumpkin-head in the first place! It gave way at last and I started running again, my bare feet slipping in the sand and the hose pulling back like a live thing. It was just like running in a night-mare.

A minute or two after the hose was connected there came the heartening hiss of water on flame, and the lurid glow began to fade. At the same moment we heard the alarm sound in the village, so we four women retired to the side-lines, on the principle that the men had everything under control and our kindest action would be to keep out from under foot. I could see Rufus in there pitching, and I exclaimed, "Dinah!" I'd forgotten all about her.

She came out of the darkness of the beach, and I was pleased to see that she'd had the intelligence to put on her bathrobe. I guess the reason that I'd forgotten her was that I'm always sure she will act with good sense, which is more than can be said of her mother. I took the two little girls over to my cottage, where they would be warm, and we watched the arrival of the Fire Department from the bedroom window. The big red trucks came clanging and screaming along the point, with spot-lights blazing and helmeted men clinging to tail and running-boards. It was very exciting and Caro almost had hysterics.

In the wake of the engines came what amounted to a parade of people. There must have been almost a hundred, and Trudy said, her big brown eyes wide, "Golly! The whole of Point Connett's coming to Our Fire!" She sounded so much like the pleased hostess of an unexpectedly successful party, or the leading lady after a terrific First Night, that I burst into laughter. It was the first time since 9:30 that I'd found anything to laugh about, and it felt good.

Just then I heard Mr. Young issuing an order. "Rufus! For the love of mike, go home and get some clothes on! *People* are coming!"

I knew what he meant. Up to that time the fire had been a family affair, and all the Angelica clan was used to seeing its members running around indecently clad. But when the Outlanders began to arrive— Well, that was a cat of two other colors. We had our pride, after all.

In a matter of seconds Rufus burst into the cottage, and I never saw such a sight. He'd lost a couple of buttons off his shorts, and they were wet and filthy. His long legs, his bare back and chest, and his pleasant face were smudged with smoke and soot, his hair was even more on end than usual, and his teeth and eye-balls glistened white and wild in the surrounding murk. He was certainly something with which to frighten children as he climbed into his dungarees.

"I've got to go right back," he announced. "We–" –*We,* yet!–"We've got it under control, but Mrs. Correia's going home to-night. So Don and I've got to help her load the cars. I told her, Ma, we'd use our car, too."

I said of course, and that being the case, the girls and I might as well go over and help, too. So we all trailed back to Correia's.

I guess I just don't understand people very well, or else the ethics of a fire in Civilization differ from those of a fire in the backwoods. Where I come from, if a neighbor has a fire, you do one of two things. If humanly possible, you dive in and help to the best of your ability. If for some reason you can't help–some reason like a bum heart or a broken arm–you just keep right away from the whole thing, in the belief that if you can't help, at least you'll try not to hinder. You certainly don't stand around in the way with your hands in your pockets.

All around Correia's house was a ring of spotless people in nice clean clothes, with their hands in their pockets. They looked pleased and entertained, and as I pushed through the crowd I actually heard an intelligent-looking man say in cultivated accents, "Well, it's a nice change from sitting around in the house all week-end, looking at TV."

Rufus was right behind me, and he muttered in my ear, "Want I should sock him, Ma?" For a moment I was sorely tempted.

But then I said, "No. What's the use? No amount of socking will teach some people decency and manners." I said it loudly and clearly, but the man obviously didn't know what I was talking about, and if he'd known, I doubt if he'd have cared. We went into the house, and to a scene of utter confusion.

The fire had started around the base of the fire-place. Because of the weather, the Correia's had had a fire going constantly for three days, and the neighboring beams had heated to the ignition point. To get at the fire, the firemen had been forced to rip out a partition and to break up the stone hearth with pick-axes, leaving a yawning hole in the floor. The place was littered with chips and broken mortar, and flooded with dirty water. It was a mess. My heart bled for Ruth when I saw her living-room rug.

In addition to all this, the firemen were still at work, and there were several unidentified persons wandering around, and one group of three men standing in the middle of the living-room floor, talking about politics and fishing. Ruth explained to me rapidly that all her bedding and the children's new school wardrobes were taking on a fire-and-water sale odor, and she thought the sooner she moved the works up to her village house, the better. I agreed, and started emptying closets and carrying the contents out to the cars. Every time I passed through the living-room, I said excuse me to the three men, and they said certainly; but they didn't offer to move.

Finally I asked Ruth in exasperation, "Who *are* those men?"

"*I* don't know," she told me with pardonable tartness. "I never laid eyes on them before in my life. And Louise, I came in a while ago and found two women opening all my closet doors and saying what nice storage space I had. I was mad, so I guess I wasn't very polite. They apologized and said they'd always wanted to see what the inside of this cottage was like. Can you tie that?" I told her quite truthfully that I could not; that I couldn't imagine going into a stranger's house and poking around under any circumstances, and that I would certainly not take advantage of misfortune to do so.

All this time firemen had been milling in and out, most of them speaking to me with an air of acquaintance. I didn't recognize any of them, although I had a feeling that I should. Suddenly it dawned on me that I knew almost all of them. They were the various citizens with whom I had come in contact two or three times a week all summer, at gas pumps and in stores and on delivery trucks. What threw me off was their helmets and rubber coats. I'd been used to seeing them in casual work clothes. After that, things became a bit more matey, and finally one said to me, "Miz Rich, you been running?"

"It seems to me, sir," I said, "that I've spent this entire night running my head off. Why?"

"Thought so. You're all perspiring. Shouldn't run like that at your age."

I put my hand to my face. I had been running, but not recently, and I felt nicely cooled off. My hand came away black and glistening, and I made a dive for the bathroom mirror. "Ruth," I howled, "why didn't you *tell* me?"

I had been, if you will remember, cold-creaming my face, when all this started. The cold cream had melted and was running goobersomely down inside the collar of the shirt that had once been white. Moreover, it had picked up every speck of soot within ten miles. Talk about Rufus' frightening children! I'd have frightened Rasputin. I looked down at my filthy shirt, my rolled-up dungarees, my bare legs and feet. It didn't help any to hear a cool, detached dame who was sight-seeing in the kitchen cabinets murmur to her companion, a smart number in a spotless white raincoat and spectator pumps, "Who *is* That Woman?"

I did the best I could with a couple of pieces of Kleenex that I swiped from Ruth's box. "Ruth," I repeated, "*why* didn't you tell me?"

She looked surprised, and then laughed. "To tell you the truth, I never noticed how you looked. I was too busy being thankful for you." That made me feel better.

Finally it was over. The Fire Department left, the morbid curiosity seekers drifted away, the Correias went back to the village, and the beach was left to darkness and the Riches and the Youngs and Rita Friedman. As I was parking my car after having taken a load of clothes to the village, Rita came out of her lighted cottage.

"I know it's one o'clock in the morning, but we can't sleep yet. We've got a huge pot of coffee on. Come on over and help us hold a post-mortem." I said there was nothing I'd like better, made sure that Dinah was a-bed and asleep, told Rufus he could come with me, and joined the party.

We sat around the table in the kitchen, Rita, her

mother and father, Rufus, and I. We drank coffee or Coke and ate rye-bread and cheese sandwiches, and hashed the whole thing over. You know how it goes.

"It was lucky it started so early, or they might have been overcome by smoke and burned in their beds."

"Wasn't Ruth wonderful! So calm and self-possessed."

"If it hadn't been for that beat-up old hose of yours, the place would have burned flat."

"You know, Louise,"—this was Mr. Young speaking—"for a kid of fourteen, Rufus did all right. He's a good boy."

Gratified beyond words, I patted my son on the knee, to his embarrassment. Then I thought of something. "Hey!" I addressed Mr. Young inelegantly. "Who was that other man under the house, and what did he think he was doing?"

Mr. Young threw back his head and hooted. "It's funny now, but it wasn't then. He's from along down the point. I don't know his name, but this I do know about him. He has a single-track mind. He came rushing up with this brand-new fire extinguisher that he bought only last Saturday. He was going to perform miracles with it; and he might have, if the thing had worked. He got right on top of the fire, aimed, got set, and phutt! Nothing happened. He got mad—don't know that I blame him; five-fifty gone up the spout—, and made up his mind that the crying thing was going to work or else. So he stuck there, right in the way, swearing and cursing and fooling with it, while Manny and I tried to shovel sand and pour water around and over him. We asked him to get the aitch out of the way, but he wouldn't. He was going to be a hero or die in the attempt."

"Why didn't you throw sand in his face?" I asked. "Nothing like a faceful of sand to cool boyish enthusiasm."

Mr. Young looked at me reproachfully. "You can't very well do a thing like that, when a guy's trying to help. It wouldn't be very nice."

I drained my coffee cup and got to my feet. "Come on, son," I said to Rufus. "We've heard everything, so let's go home to bed. *Nice.* When the house is burning down over your head! Just remember this day and hour, my boy. You have for once come in contact with a true gentleman."

After Labor Day the beach was marvelous. There wasn't a soul on it except me, and on week-ends, my children. I went into Walsh's one afternoon, and Mr. Walsh asked with some surprise, "*You* still here?"

"Yup," I said. "Until the end of the month."

"Best time of the year," he told me. "This and October. Summer season can't hold a candle to the fall." He sacked up my groceries. "We'll kind of miss you when you're gone."

"Why, Mr. Walsh!" I exclaimed, genuinely pleased and touched. "Thank you!" I meant it. In my old role of Maine Native, I like the summer people, but I was always a little glad to see them go. I had never told one of them that I would miss her.

I had a lovely time alone on Angelica during September, and I even finished my book. There is something very special about getting up in the morning and looking along a mile crescent of pale gold sand, and knowing that it is all yours; that the only foot-prints that will mar its tide-smoothed perfection during the day will be your own and your dog's. It gives you a sort of Robinson Crusoe feeling, a feeling of self-sufficiency and spiritual symmetry.

When there are too many people around for too long a time, I grow out of shape, like an apple that grows against a twig. Living alone on Angelica all that month took the dents out of me. In the evening, Caro and I would walk the whole length of the point; and I loved to look back from the outermost, surf-washed rock and see on all the long stretch of darkening beach only one light gleaming, my own.

All right, all right. My friends, too, think I am queer.

Eventually, of course, September came to an end. We had to go back to Bridgewater for good. It was a sad, sad day. Remember those two young characters who told me way back in the winter that they didn't want to go to the beach? That they knew they wouldn't like it? You should have seen them on that last day. Talk about long faces! They went about looking as though there had been a triple death in the family and saying, "But can't we come back *part* of next summer? Gee, Ma, we *like* it here. Gee whiz, you're *mean*."

My own face wasn't any too short. Gee whiz, I liked it, too. I derived a little comfort from the knowledge that for once Mother had been Right. Her judgment in the matter of a summer at the beach had been correct. I'm afraid I rubbed it in a little.

Then, too, I had a problem on my hands, which helped to keep my mind off my sorrows. It was this: How in the world can you come to the beach with one car-load of possessions, wear out and throw away half of them in the course of the season, and end with two car-loads to take back? I would have sworn that I hadn't made one major purchase, and certainly the shell collection didn't take up ten cubic feet. Oh, well, that is one of the sweet mysteries of Life.

The kids are talking already about going to a dude ranch year-after-next. Heaven help the Only Parent! But I can tell you one thing, anyhow. No one repeat no one is going to get *me* onto a horse!

CHAPTER ELEVEN

Dinah's New York

IT seems to me that I always have my neck out. I'm always making promises for the future, unwarrantably convinced that to-day is to-day, and we'll deal with it; and to-morrow won't come. I ought to have learned by now that inevitably to-morrow does come, and I'm going to have to fulfill my fine promises.

Take for example the summer when Rufus was ten. He came to me and asked me when I was going to teach him to drive a car. I said off-hand, because I was deep in a who-dun-it, "When you are as tall as I am." I was very sure that by that time I would have died of old age and someone else would be saddled with the White Woman's Burden. Or else— Oh, what a fool I am!—he'd have forgotten about the whole thing. So I went happily and obliviously about my business, all unaware of the close and calculating scrutiny of my son.

When he was eleven, he came to me again. "Take off your shoes, Ma," he said, "and let's stand back to back in front of the mirror."

Of course I'd forgotten my stipulation ten minutes after I'd uttered it, so I didn't see much point in this nonsense. But I was feeling good-natured, and if it would make the kid happy, I'd string along with him. I kicked off my loafers and stood as tall as I could against him. He topped me by half an inch, and I'm no shrimp.

"Ha!" he said in a satisfied tone. "When do we start the driving lessons?"

It all came back to me in a sickening flash. Had I been living in any civilized community, I could have countered self-righteously by saying, "You know that it's against the State Law for you even to *touch* the wheel of a car until you're sixteen," or whatever the age happened to be in that locality. But the Carry Road is different. Just a rough woods-road, it runs only from one lake to another, a distance of about five miles, and it gives no access to the Outside. The only cars on it are the Miller's, the Parsons', and mine. There was no reason at all why a boy of eleven shouldn't drive along it, if his mother was fool enough to let him. No one would even raise an eyebrow.

I know when I'm licked, so I scuffed my loafers back on. "Now is as good a time as any," I told him philosophically, and accompanied him out into the clearing where the jallopy was parked. I explained the starter, the choke, the gear shift, and the brake, to his intense impatience. He knew all about that from observation, he told me.

"OK, then, Smarty-pants, get in and start driving," I said.

We rounded the corner by the woodshed on two wheels and crashed into a boulder by the side of the road. Rufus leaped out with the announcement that he guessed he didn't care about learning to drive to-day.

"Oh, no, you don't, my fine-feathered friend," I told him, fingering my ribs in an effort to determine how many had been cracked, while at the same time trying to light a cigarette for nonchalance sake. "You climb right back in here. You started this, and you're going to finish it." He got in, and we made a halting and perilous trip to Middle Dam, off the Carry more than we were on it.

Three days later he had practically mastered the art of driving. Isn't it marvelous to be young and teachable? I let him drive me up to Middle on the fourth evening, and asked him to back the car around while I went in and collected the milk and the mail. In the accomplishing of this mission, I encountered my friend, Swene Meisener, who works for the Parsons.

"Hi, Swene," I said. "Get an eyeful of Rufus out there. He can already drive better than I can."

"Wal, that's good," Swene said in his deep and deliberate voice. He thought for a moment. "Not that that's sayin' much," he added dispassionately.

That certainly put me in my place.

When Rufus was ten, I took him to New York. The minute we got back, Dinah started hounding me about when was I going to take her to New York, gee whiz, it wasn't fair. Rufus could do everything and go everywhere, while she just stayed home and never had any fun at all.

"Dear," I said, "you must remember that Rufus is five years older than you are. When you get to be a big girl, ten years old and in the Fifth Grade, I'll take you to New York." There was a certain amount of muttering, but she finally accepted my pronouncement, and I relaxed. Five years is a long time, and anything can happen during the period.

But if you think she forgot, you're crazy. Last fall she started in again. "I'm in the Fifth Grade. I'll be ten in March. So you've got to take me to New York this winter. You *promised,* Ma. You said when I was ten and in the Fifth Grade—" Dinah and elephants! I was stuck with my story, and I knew it.

I said all right, darn it, we'd go to New York; and we might just as well get it over with. We'd go a little before Christmas, so she could see the Christmas displays; and in the meanwhile she could be making up a list of the things she wanted to do and see. "There are a few things I want to attend to," I added. "I want to see Mr. Wing and Mr. Carrick and Miss Fish and Mrs. Sias. Miss Fish has invited us to lunch whenever we go, and—"

"Oh, Ma, no! If you get together with all those people, it'll be yak-yak-yak for hours. That's no fun for me, and this is supposed to be my trip. I don't want us to see anybody except just Aunt Alice."

"All right, all *right!*" I told her. "I have to see Mr. Wing and Miss Fish on business. We'll do that the first thing Friday morning. Then if you're a good girl and sit quietly while I'm transacting my business, the rest of the week-end we'll do what you want to do."

"Can we eat on the train? Can we stay in a hotel? I've never eaten on a train or stayed in a hotel. I want to go to the Zoo, and the top of the Empire State Building. Did you know that's the tallest building in the world, Ma? And I want to see the Statue of Liberty and ride in a subway. I've never been in a subway. Can we—?"

"Yes, yes, *yes,*" I said, tired out already from simply

thinking about it. "Put the most important things at the top of your list, because we might not have time to do everything you want. I can't promise," I said, getting smart in my old age, "to cover the whole list; and anyhow, there are a couple of surprises I'm saving for you that I think you'll enjoy. *If* you're a good girl and behave yourself like a lady," I added, striving to retain a precarious whip-hand.

"Oh, I *will* be good, Mummy," she breathed, and went off to pack her suitcase, although this expedition was three weeks in the future. I'm sure I need not add that the suitcase was packed and unpacked forty-seven times before we actually took off.

The trip started out propitiously. When we went into the dining car and ordered our lunch, Dinah, unable to contain herself, confided to the waitress that this was the first time in all her life that she'd eaten in a train, and that she and her mother were going to the top of the Empire State Building, and that she'd never been to New York before. Pretty soon the hostess came along with two candy bars. She said that she understood that the little girl was on her first trip to the city, and she hoped she'd have a wonderful time. The New York, New Haven, & Hartford Railroad, she said, would like to contribute the candy bars toward making her trip pleasant. I opened my mouth to say that that was very nice of them, but Dinah forestalled me.

"Oh, thank you! Oh, aren't people *kind*, Mummy?" She opened her shoulder purse and stashed away the candy bars. "I'm going to take them home to my brother. Poor dope, he has to go to school to-day and to-morrow, so he ought to have some reward, don't you think, while my mother and I are having a good time?" The hostess said she did think so, and I reflected that, no credit to me, I had a nice daughter with proper instincts.

I had made reservations at the Algonquin, because I like it there. Besides, while I am perfectly capable of dealing with the perils of the backwoods, such as blizzards, bears, forest fires, floods, and other assorted dangers, I'm a pretty weak sister in a city. It's so big and noisy and crowded; and I get lost, and take wrong subways, and find myself crossing against lights, so that my sanity, if not my life, is continually endangered. The Algonquin is small enough, and I've stayed there often enough, so that it seems like a veritable sanctuary in a howling wilderness. In the taxi, I told Dinah to straighten her hat and put on her gloves, since when we checked into hotels, we tried to look halfway respectable.

"Stay right near me," I instructed her, "and be quiet and good." She composed her face into the butter-wouldn't-melt-in-my-mouth expression of all little girls on their best behavior.

It didn't last long. I asked the man at the desk if it would be possible for me to rent a small portable radio, so that my little girl could listen to some of her favorite programs in the evening. He said that it would. "But," he added, "I don't think it will really be necessary. The room we've given you has a television set."

Dinah's hard-won composure flew into a thousand bits. "Oh Mummy!" she cried. "A TV set in our very own room! Oh, boy! Now I'm really living!"

Of course that would be the moment when one of those strange silences had fallen over the lobby. All the smartly dressed women and suave gentlemen with flowers in their button-holes seated at the little tables with cocktails in their well-groomed hands were as quiet and motionless as illustrations in a rotogravure section. These silences, when the cat has got everyone's tongue, are supposed to occur at either twenty minutes of, or twenty minutes past, the hour. Of course, that's silly. It's unreasonable and impossible. But do you know, whenever I think to check, it does seem to work out that way.

On this occasion, at twenty minutes past six, Dinah's ecstatic voice penetrated to the furthermost corner, and a shout of laughter went up. She blushed a painful scarlet, and I was sorry for the poor little girl, trying so hard to be good. Then the bell captain stepped forward. "Is this your daughter, Mrs. Rich? We're glad to have you with us again. If there is anything I can do to make your stay pleasant—"

"Thank you, Paul. I'm glad to be here, too," I told him.

Dinah forgot her embarrassment. "Do you know *everybody?*" she asked, impressed.

I said that I did not, by a long shot; but this happened to be a hotel at which I stayed often before, and that I was pleased to be remembered.

"Oh, is this the place where they have the cat and the special cat door so he can get up-stairs? Can I see it?"

The bell-hop who had our luggage volunteered that the cat had Passed On, but the door was still there, if the little girl wanted to see it. And there it was, sure enough, with the name Rusty over it.

Dinah said in tones of utter amazement, "You were telling the truth, Ma! Us kids always thought that was just one of your stories."

And that's a fine reputation to have with your young, I must say.

There is a school of thought, subscribed to largely by the sentimental childless, that one of the joys of parenthood is the opportunity to do what is known as keeping young with your children. In my opinion, this is so much eye-wash. I am not young, and having mothered a dozen children wouldn't restore my belief in Santa Claus, or make these aged bones and muscles more limber and supple, or give back to me the conviction that black is black and white is white and there are no possible shadings of gray. Actually, that would be a very undesirable state of affairs. I have spent several decades working toward a certain maturity, which I'll admit I have not completely achieved, and I have no wish to return to the bright halls of youth. Youth is hard and easily hurt, supplied with a set of iron convictions, most of them mistaken, beset by doubts and fears of things that should be neither doubted nor feared, possessed of overwhelming confidence in frail reeds, and in general a period of such unreality and confusion that I wonder anyone ever survives it. I don't want to keep young with my children; and even if I did and it were possible, I'd be doing them no favor. Some one around here has to have a little horse sense, some ballasting qualities, to possess even a limited fund of experience on which to draw in an emergency, has to give the illusion, at least, of solidity and security.

The few beliefs that I retain from my own youth will probably last as long as I do. They've been subject to hard wear and tear for quite a while now. As for the rest, the beliefs in fairy god-mothers and magic castles and Prince Charmings and Sleeping Beauties, they have gone and I am glad of it. I've got something better in their place. Now I know that it is much more satisfactory to work for what you want than to have someone wave it out of the air for you with a magic wand; that real people are a thousand times more interesting and likable than all the shining royalty in Grimm's; and that no crystal palace ever devised by Anderson could compare in wonder and beauty with the world around us and the earth beneath our feet.

No, I don't even try to keep young with my children. The nearest I have come to it recently was purely involuntary, when I had whooping cough and mumps last winter, right along with them. It was not a very enlightening or rewarding experience.

But in spite of all I have just been saying, sharing a new experience with a child is refreshing and a little saddening. You can't go back, but you get a brief, reminding glimpse of what it was like to be a child, and you are saddened by remembrance of the painful stripping away of illusion after illusion. I do not consider myself world-weary. At least, I hope I am not. Even so, a hotel room, no matter how nice, is still to me just another hotel room. I certainly take for granted a closet with a light that goes on when you open the door, a tiled bath and shower, a desk supplied with hotel stationary, reading lamps over the beds, and a telephone. While I wouldn't demand it for my own amusement, I can take even a TV set more or less in my stride, as long as I am not required to turn it on and look at it. A hotel room, in short, is not to me the guest-room in heaven.

It was obviously just that to Dinah. For about thirty seconds she was speechless, pretty nearly a record for her. Then she flew around opening doors and drawers and turning on water taps and lights and the TV set. She unpacked our few belongings and put them away neatly, and then leaned out the window.

"There's some iron stairs right outside here," her voice floated back in, "and the people next door have a box on it. I'm going to see—"

Before I could grab her, she was out on the fire escape, investigating.

"They've got some cream and butter and lettuce and cheese—"

"You come right straight back in here," I snarled. "What if you should fall? What if those people should catch you looking in their box? They'd complain to the hotel, and the hotel wouldn't let us stay here any longer." I wasn't sure that this was true, but it seemed a time for sweeping statements. "Now wash your face and hands," I directed her when she reappeared, somewhat chastened, "and we'll go down to dinner. Then maybe we can take a little walk over to Times Square, so you can see all the lights and the people."

"Do we *have* to? I'm not hungry, and anyhow, I can eat Rufus' candy bars and get him some more to-morrow. Can't I stay here? Please? Gee, I've never had a shower, and I want to take one right now. And another before I go to bed. And I want to write post-cards to Rufus and Granny and Pauline and Rainey and— You said the cards in the desk were for us to use. And I want to go in the closet and shut the door and see if the light really does go out, like you said. And I want to look at TV, and—"

After all, she was only nine, and it was the first time she'd ever stayed in a hotel. I couldn't share her delight and enthusiasm. I was too old. But I could remember now,

"There's some iron stairs right outside here," her voice floated back in, "and the people next door have a box on it. I'm going to see—" Before I could grab her, she was out on the fire escape, investigating.

dimly and vaguely, what it had been like to be nine and new to the world.

"All right," I said. "We'll stay here. We'll have dinner sent up and eat it right in this room. Wait till you see it. They have a table all set, with a white cloth and glasses and silver, that they wheel in; and they bring the food in a little oven with a flame under it, to keep it hot."

She looked at me in silence. Then she said, "Ma, in the morning I'll make the beds all by myself. You won't have to do a thing. I'll wash out the tub and hang all the towels up neatly."

And suddenly I loved her so much that I couldn't spoil it for her by telling her about the maid service. Bless her heart, she was doing the best she knew how to thank me for taking her to New York. There'd be time enough in the morning to explain about the maid.

She took three showers that evening before she finally went to sleep, and wrapped the left-over roll in a newspaper and hid it in the waste-basket, so that the feelings of the nice man who had brought us up our dinner wouldn't be hurt. She didn't want him to think we didn't appreciate the trouble he'd taken. I let her do it, too. She'd grow thoughtless like all the rest of us adults soon enough, without any help from me.

My last coherent recollection of events during that week-end in New York is of my call on my publishers. That made sense. My editor and I sat in a quiet office and talked business reasonably, while Dinah, true to her promise, looked at a picture book and acted like a lady. After that, everything is slightly out of focus. This was New York, all right, but it was no New York I'd ever seen before, and I'll probably never see it again, since the chances of my taking another nine-year-old daughter there on her first visit are exceedingly slim.

I remember being at the top of the Empire State Building, where the wind was blowing a gale. The city lay spread out before and below us, with people running like ants along the streets. We could see the Statue of Liberty, misty and gray and small, but somehow impressive, over in the harbor. That was the only time during our stay that I was comfortably cool. Although it was the middle of December, New York was having a heat wave, and I spent the rest of the week-end running around with my tongue hanging out like a dog's. The next minute, or so it seemed, we were in Woolworth's basement, buying a lethal weapon called a Ray Gun. This was a plastic revolver, and when you snapped it, a coil of paper shot out to a distance of about four feet, and your victim presumably dropped dead. We walked up Fifth Avenue leaving a swath of corpses in our wake, including those of two traffic cops and a boy whose face Dinah didn't care for; and a woman in a mink cape asked us where we'd bought that toy. She was looking for something for her grandson, aged nine, and did Dinah think he'd like that? Dinah quietly exterminated a taxi driver, and said that she herself was nine, and she *loved* her Ray Gun. We'd bought it in the cellar of that store right over there, and it cost a whole twenty-nine cents, plus tax. The woman thanked us and disappeared into Woolworth's maw.

Then we were in Central Park, looking for the carousel, which was one of the surprises I'd had in mind for Dinah. We almost never did get to it, though, because in our search we had to pass the zoo. Did I say pass? Fat chance I had of getting my animal-mad child away until she had personally greeted each individual beast there. I kept telling her that we were going with Aunt Alice to a much better zoo to-morrow, and she kept shushing me. It wasn't the fault of these animals that their zoo wasn't as nice as the Bronx Zoo, she told me, and their feelings would be terribly hurt if they overheard my remarks. We had to linger interminably in front of each cage, to avoid any appearance of uncivil haste. But we finally did get to the carousel.

And here we bogged down again. My naive idea had been that we'd just go over and look at it and take one ride. After all, in my book one ride on a merry-go-round is exactly like another ride on a merry-go-round and drains the cup of merry-go-riding experience to the dregs. But since I had not managed to keep young with my child, I had forgotten how to imbue each gracefully carved and gaudily painted horse with a personality of its own. I had lost the ability to become intoxicated by the gay, thin tinkle of the music and the swoop and swerve of the plunging steeds. I just got dizzy and slightly sea-sick. So I said that I guessed that would be enough of that, and let's go back to the hotel and rest before dinner.

"Oh, Ma, *no!* I want to ride every single horse here, and especially that black one with the gold mane and silver hoofs. His name is Midnight. That's what I've named him. I *have* to ride him! He's looking right straight at me, and he knows me."

"You can't ride every horse," I said firmly. "You can have three more rides, and then we'll have to go. Only three more, so pick out the three horses you like best. I," I added, "won't go this time. I'll just sit here on the bench and watch you ride." And that's what I did, while Dinah went round and round to the music, her face bemused and glowing.

It was nice there in the park in the sun, with the music playing and the lovely, improbable horses galloping and galloping endlessly after each other, while all the little children with shining eyes rode as in a dream. Far away the noise of the traffic on either side of the park sounded like distant surf, and it was like being on an island where everything was always going to be beautiful and perfect, and no one was ever going to grow old and worried and tired.

There was a sudden swift clatter of feet and the discordant note of rough voices speaking fast and tough. A wave of dark boys with hard eyes and old faces swept onto the terrace where I was sitting, and I got up. I had read only the week before about the gangs of hoodlums in their teens who conducted lightning swift raids upon the innocent and defenseless in the jungle of the city. I didn't know what I could do against them, but I did know that someone was going to get awfully hurt if they laid one finger upon my child. Probably I read too much and believe too much of what I read.

I was unprepared for what happened. They bought their tickets, these tight-lipped, sharp-eyed savages, and when the carousel slowed to a stop and the music faded into silence, they swarmed through the gate and mounted, lengthening stirrups and settling themselves into the saddles. The bell rang, the horses started slowly to rise and fall and plunge, gathering speed as the music quickened; and all the boys smiled and patted the arched necks of their steeds, or slapped rumps and yodelled "Hi-yo." Hard and tough and wise beyond their years they might be, but right now they were just a bunch of kids playing cowboy, pounding over some vast plain of their imaginations in pursuit of what high adventure I didn't know. They were just like any of the kids I knew back home, only perhaps a little less self-conscious about playing a childish game, and a little pathetic, too. I felt so good about it that I let Dinah have an extra ride on a white horse with a black tail and flaring crimson nostrils. His name was Fearless, she told me, and he'd been born in a box canyon up in the High Sierras.

I tore her away from there by saying that I'd just remembered a wonderful store near-by, where they sold nothing but toys, floors and floors of them, like nothing she'd ever dreamed of. So we went over to Schwartz on Fifth Avenue, and the only reason we aren't still there is that the store closed and they put us out. It was just as well. If we'd stayed any longer, we'd have had to hitch-hike home with our extravagant purchases. As it was, all we bought was a marionette, a simply fascinating affair. We had a dinner date with my sister, anyhow, to plan our campaign for the next day. While we were waiting for her, Dinah showed the bell-boys and clerk her new marionette, which in congress assembled they decided should be named Algonquin Schwartz, and told them all about Her Day and our plans for the morrow. In return she was advised that the birds in the Bronx Zoo were pretty dull and uninteresting, but she should be sure to see the snakes, monkeys, and elephants. My sister arrived just before they all got around to showing each other their vaccination scars.

People have been telling me for years that sometime when I was in New York I should go to the Bronx Zoo, because it really was Something; and for years I've been saying yes, I know, some time I really must take time to go up there. But of course I never had, and I probably never would have, if it hadn't been for Dinah. All the way to the Bronx on the subway—Dinah did get her subway ride, and decided what I could have told her, that she didn't like subways—we studied a guide book to the Zoo that my sister brought along for our convenience. She has both written books for children about animals, and edited similar books other people have written, so she is very familiar with the Zoo. She's been there a lot, getting information and checking detail. She and the guide book between them convinced us that we'd better take the advice of the personnel of the Algonquin and forget about the birds altogether. Monkeys, snakes, and elephants, yes. I said I wanted to see the big cats, because they fascinated me; and Dinah said she wanted to see a zebra, a giraffe, and the seals. Alice said we must see the penguins, because we'd love them so; and she had to take another look at the parasol ants, for professional reasons. Then if possible, she'd like to find the Slow Loris. She'd just learned about them, and she'd decided that she wanted to be one in her next incarnation.

"And what may a Slow Loris be?" I asked ignorantly.

The Slow Loris, it turned out, is a very low-grade primate, that never moves a muscle unless it absolutely has to. It eats leaves, and often spends its whole life in the same tree, although if the leaf supply runs out and it decides that life is just possibly worth living after all, it will bestir itself sufficiently to move to the next tree. "And that's what I want to do," my sister concluded. "Just find a place and sit and sit and sit, with nothing on my mind and nowhere I have to go."

I could see what she meant, after only a day and a half in the city. She lives there all the time, and the very thought exhausted me. So I told her that I guessed I'd be a Slow Loris next time, too. She said that was No Fair. She had an option on the Slow Loris. I'd have to find an animal of my own to be. I accepted this as a reasonable rule of the game, and we spent the rest of the ride marking up the map of the Zoo with a blunt pencil, for step-economy's sake. We'd start at the penguin house, we decided.

I guess we saw everything we wanted to see, except a giraffe. They'd been taken inside for the winter, and by the time we'd covered everything else, our feet were worn off to the ankle bone, and we couldn't face finding out where their winter quarters were, and then walking to wherever it was. Dinah had announced that in her next life she was going to be a penguin, because they seemed to have so much fun. She beat me on the draw by about ten seconds. I almost decided on a green-eyed black panther, because he was so handsome and lithe and graceful, attributes which it would be a delightful novelty for me to possess, I felt. I'm glad I didn't. The next week I read in TIME about the Abominable Snowman. That's what I'm going to be: a wild individualist.

We fed pop-corn to the elephants, and fish to the seals. We shuddered in horrid fascination at the big snakes, and hung entranced over the parasol ants, bustling to and fro across a bridge over a moat, their bright parasols of red and yellow and white rose petals held over their busy heads. We were interested to see that even the ant family has its goldbricks. There was a little stinker there that ran around like mad, creating the effect of labor; but actually he didn't do a thing except get into the way of his more conscientious brothers.

We admired the electric eel, and marveled that the deadly piranha could look so much like any innocuous little fish in any little brook. In short, we acted like people visiting the Zoo, even to the eating of hot dogs, and the sudden decision that we were dying on our feet and had better go home and lie down. The Bronx Zoo really is a wonderful place; but it's an awfully big place, too. I hadn't walked so far in one day for years and years.

Back in our room, we took off our shoes, ordered up cold drinks, and relaxed. Then we began really to appreciate the Zoo. As our strength returned, we regained our enthusiasm for the elephants, and remembered how sweet the little gazelles had been. My sister decided, when pressed, that she could endure our society for a while longer—after all, the poor woman had been exposed to us since nine in the morning—, so we had dinner sent up. While we were waiting for it to appear, Dinah turned on the TV to a station which apparently does nothing all day long except run off ancient horse operas, and instructed Alice and me in the Code of the West.

We were very much edified to learn that you could tell the Goodies from the Baddies, even if like us you came in on the middle of the film, when two men were throwing each other over a table in the center of what seemed to be the living-room of an elderly couple, cowering in the corners. The Goodies always wear light shirts, and the Baddies wear black. We also learned that the hero, in this case Gene Autry, would not get the girl, because he never did.

He was just straightening out a friend's romance, from sheer good-will. He wouldn't even get to kiss the girl. The only thing he ever kissed was his horse, a state of affairs that Dinah seemed to find eminently satisfactory; so I guess that the powers behind the cowboy sagas do know what they're doing.

Gene faded out down the sunset trail, strumming his guitar and singing a melancholy song, and his place was taken by Hopalong, starring in, as far as Alice and I could determine, exactly the same story that Gene had tied up so neatly in a bow-knot. Dinah was indignant when we commented on this, since even the veriest idiot ought to know that Gene's horse was Champion and Hopalong's horse was Topper, and that made all the difference. At this juncture, dinner arrived, and Dinah, to prove her point, I suppose, addressed the waiter. "What's the name of Hopalong Cassidy's horse?"

He didn't look too surprised, since by now he and Dinah were old friends of two days' standing. "Topper, of course. What's the name of Straight Arrow's horse?"

"Fury," Dinah told him immediately. "What's the name of the Lone Ranger's horse?"

Alice and I, who had been lost in the fog, shrieked together, "Silver!" That one at least we did know.

"All right," said the waiter. "What's the name of his friend and companion Tonto's horse?"

Alice and I returned to our morass of ignorance, but Dinah answered promptly, "Scout. What's the name of Roy Roger's horse?"

"Trigger." The waiter finished serving the dinner and started for the door, laughing at our silly game.

"Just a moment," my sister said. "What was the name of Alexander the Great's horse?"

The waiter opened the door and stood with his hand on the knob. His timing was perfect. "Bellerophon," he said quietly, and closed the door gently behind him, leaving us with our jaws dropped clear down onto our chests.

We were so set up by this demonstration of erudition, and also, probably, by an excellent dinner, that our strength returned to us two-fold. Our feet even stopped hurting. We put our shoes back on and went up to Rockefeller Center to see the Christmas Tree, the biggest and grandest that either Dinah or I had ever viewed. We watched the people skating on the rink, and Dinah decided that New York was wonderful.

"Because, Aunt Alice," she said, "this afternoon we were simply boiling on the Plains of Africa up at the Zoo; and now we're watching people skate on real ice. Is it always like this in New York, Auntie?"

My sister allowed as how it was, pretty nearly; that was why she liked living there. Dinah pondered that for a while, and then announced that she guessed she'd still rather live in the country. Her mother's own daughter. I can't understand my sister. We have exactly the same background of small town; but she is urban and I am hick. She is sophisticated and I'm simple. Oh, well—

The next morning, Sunday, Dinah and I had planned to go to the Statue of Liberty, the sole item of unfinished business on her list. But we awoke to a down-pour, a wet, gray, mean day. So we decided to skip Liberty. We'd seen her already in the distance. Possibly, I told Dinah, she wouldn't be so handsome, near-to. Very likely the stairs we'd have to climb would be dirty, with chewing-gum wrappers in the corners. Dinah proved amenable.

I have a theory that things should stop before you expect them to, if you're going to retain a pleasant memory of them. School Committees should announce that school is going to close on Wednesday, June 23, let us say; and then at the end of the session on Friday, June 18, the pupils should be told that this is It: they need not return until September. And people should be called back from their vacations a day or so sooner than they had planned. The tail-end of any experience, when your body is in one world, but your mind has gone ahead to another, is pretty unsatisfactory. So I wasn't too dashed by the necessity of cutting short this week-end in New York. I turned my whole mind to the problem of getting back to Massachusetts as soon as possible; and five hours on a train didn't appeal particularly to me.

"Dinah," I said, trying to sneak up on the subject, "you'd like to get back to your grandmother's as fast as you can, wouldn't you? So that you can tell all the kids about New York, before you forget anything."

She said that she would.

"Well," I told her, "if we fly back, it'll only take an hour or less to get to Boston. You'll have plenty of time, before bed-time—"

She turned on me a set and stubborn look. She had flown twice from Maine to Massachusetts, and been airsick on both occasions. After the second she had announced categorically that no one, ever, was going to get her off the ground again.

"You won't be sick this time," I assured her hastily. "The planes on this run are much bigger and don't bounce around so much. It'll be just like riding on the train, only we'll get there quicker." I looked at her uncompromising face. "I'll tell you what I'll do. I'll give you fifty cents if you're not sick."

She thought it over. Fifty cents was an awful lot of money. For fifty cents she could do almost anything, even refrain from throwing up her boot heels. "All right," she said, and started putting things into the suitcases.

An hour and a half later we were over Boston, both in the best of health and spirits. I tidied Dinah's hair and drew on my gloves, while Dinah began making a mental catalogue of all the things she had to do the minute she got home. She had to give Grammy and Rufus the boxes of candy we'd bought them, and run over to the Haskells and Farrells and Atwoods with the little gifts she'd got for their children, and if there was still time, hop on her bike and take Miss Folsom's present over to her, and—

At this point the stewardess bent over us. "We're not landing for a few minutes," she said. "The ceiling is so low that they're taking us down at longer intervals than usual, and we'll have to wait our turn. It won't be long, but can I get either of you anything? Some coffee or hot chocolate? Or some cookies or a sandwich?"

I said no thank you, but Dinah said she'd like some cookies and a hot chocolate. It arrived, rich and dark and topped with whipped-cream. I regarded it with some misgivings.

I could have saved myself the worry. For two solid hours we circled the airport, with nothing to look at except each other, the other passengers in the plane, the gray wall of the clouds outside the little window, and, occasionally, other planes—there were six of us stacked up over

Logan—doing the same thing we were doing at different levels. It was of no particular comfort to me that Rocky Marciano was in the same fix we were, but it may have been to Dinah. At any rate, during this interval she drank three more hot chocolates and ate at least a pound of cookies, some of them filled with a nauseous pink marshmallow, without the slightest repercussions. I was the one who became slightly queasy, just from watching her, although not, luckily, to the point of disaster. I think that from now on we will consider Dinah's famous tendency to air-sickness an exploded myth.

We finally got home so late and were so tired that we both went right to bed without even thinking of calling on any neighbors. And that ended the trip to New York.

It was fun, and I'm glad we took it, but I hope we don't have to go through it all again. I don't imagine that we will. Any parent knows that the young have very fertile minds when it comes to thinking up new and gruelling experiences for their progenitors. The Only Parent has just one advantage over the others. She is spared any uncertainty as to who is going to be elected to conduct the next safari, any false hope that when it comes to the two week trip into Canada, or the visit to Washington, D.C., it'll be her turn to stay home with a good book, resting.

It's a thought that seduces me with its quiet and peaceful connotations; or it would if I didn't know that I'd be on pins and needles the whole time, wondering just how much I was missing.

CHAPTER TWELVE

As It Is

THIS then is what it means to be an Only Parent. It is exactly like being any other parent, multiplied by much more than two, since the progression is not mathematical at all. It is a matter of combining the roles of mother, father, wage-earner, homekeeper, and sometimes—and I do not mean to seem irreverent—almost of God. It means being regarded, always at the moments when you are most painfully aware of your fallibility, as infallible; and at the times when you know with an absolute knowledge that you are right, as being a silly, old-fashioned type who has failed to keep abreast of modern thinking and up-to-date trends. For me at least it has meant living in places where you never intended to live, doing things you never planned to do, undergoing experiences you never had any wish to undergo, simply because your own wishes and plans and intentions no longer come first. Do you think for one minute that, had I been a free agent, I would ever have touched a snake with a ten foot pole? Or spent whole afternoons playing Pounce? Or belonged to the PTA? Or left the place I love and call home to spend winter after winter in a semi-suburb? Ha! You can think again.

And what do you get out of all this business?

You get a lot of expense and worry and trouble. You lose a lot of sleep, and you raise a lot of blisters, and you develop a lot of gray hair and wrinkles. That must be pretty clear to the most casual observer; and even the most casual observer would be completely justified in concluding that the whistle isn't worth the penny.

But he'd be wrong. There are rewards in parenthood that are invisible to the eye of any but the parent, or, I suppose, the truly dedicated teacher of the young. This is a statement which, in the days when I was free as a feather on the breeze, was often made to me by those of my contemporaries who had married young and started families. I took it with more than a grain of salt. I knew a case of sour grapes when I saw one, I was sure. I myself had occasionally been known to wax enthusiastic over a bad bargain, out of pure, stiff-necked pride. They couldn't fool me!

But they did fool me, just the same, because what they said was true.

I suppose the most obvious reward of parenthood compares roughly with the satisfaction a gardener gets out of producing a crop of corn, or a stone mason out of building a wall, or a musician out of composing a melody. From basic material—a handful of seed, a pile of rock, a showering of bird notes in the dawn, or the few pounds of flesh and bone and blood and common reflexes that are a baby—he has built and shaped and developed something to stand in his name. It may be good, or it may be bad; but good or bad, it is his creation, bearing his stamp. The corn may go to waste, the wall may fall down, the song may be forgotten, the man may turn out useless; but the weeks or months or years of working and planning and dreaming will never be lost to the creator. They are of the fabric of his life, both his substance and his shaper. And if the corn nourishes life, the wall stands, the song is remembered, the man be strong, then indeed may he say to himself, "My life has been turned to good account."

There is another less tangible reward in parenthood. I have written of the places I have lived, the things I have done, the persons I have known, the geographical and sweat-and-sinew side of Only Parenthood. There is another realm, the realm of the spirit and the imagination, that is open to the adult only through close and constant and loving association with the child. The adult ordinarily has outgrown and put away childish things. To him the gates of Magic are closed. He no longer trails clouds of glory; and those who retain in the body of a man the mind of a child are rightfully considered to be dangerously incompetent to deal with the world. But there is a special dispensation bestowed upon parents. On the one hand they are given a terrible and frightening responsibility, so that they must at least attempt to be always wiser and calmer and stronger than it is their true nature to be; and then, in recompense, they are allowed to glimpse again the world of small things, of wonder and delight. For a moment, on a clear and quiet evening, they may believe again in the spell of wishing on the first star, hanging glimmering and far in an apple-green sky; or trust in the efficacy to ward off misfortune of a white-banded lucky stone, carried secretly in a pocket and cool to the touch of the hand.

I owe my children much more than they owe me.

When Rufus was very small, he found a heap of fresh-water mussel shells by a muskrat (only here we call them mushrats) burrow. When he brought them home to play with, he asked me what they were. Probably I should have seized upon the occasion to give a Natural History lesson, but I was busy, so I didn't. I told him they were shells, and let it go at that. He was perfectly satisfied, so why should I jump in all over, I excused myself. At that age, when almost everything is new and strange, it seems to be enough to have a name to put to an object. I guess it's reassuring to learn that enough other people have observed any given phenomenon in the vast and confusing universe around one's small self to have a word for it. I imagine—because I have forgotten what it was like when I was that age—that it would make you feel less alone in your explorations and discoveries, to find that others had been before you.

At any rate, Rufus played happily with the shells for a while. Then one day he came in with starry, excited eyes and a lard pail full of water, at the bottom of which two live mussels reposed. "Look, Ma!" he exclaimed. "I found some more shells, and they've got little people in them!"

I said yes, the shells were the houses of the little people. That was where they lived. They could open the doors when they wanted something to eat or some fresh water; but if danger came, they could slam their doors shut tight.

"What became of the Little People in the other houses that I play with?" he wanted to know; and I told him that I guessed the muskrats ate them.

"Did it hurt them?" he demanded fearfully, and I told him that I didn't think so, since they had no nervous systems that I knew anything about. And anyhow, I added, it didn't matter. They were only mussels.

"But they're *alive!*" he reminded me, in the tone of one launching a terrible indictment.

I was licked and I knew it. It would take a more able intellect than mine to explain just where the line was to be drawn between life that is sacred and life that is not. The mere fact of life, even in a mussel, was to him a mystery and a miracle, as I suppose it should be to all of us. Somewhere along the way I had lost sight of that fact, and I was glad to have it recalled to my attention. All of us need reminders of that sort. We fall all too easily into the attitude that because people live far away and have a different pigmentation from ours, we needn't trouble our minds and hearts about their fates.

One Sunday afternoon last winter, while we were in Bridgewater, I lost Dinah. At least, I didn't know where she was, although she probably was oriented, so shouldn't be termed lost. Still and all, I like to have a rough idea as to the whereabouts, occupations, and companions of my children; so I started driving around looking for her. I found her kneeling on the dirty side-walk—in her good coat, too—in front of the A&P, with her face pressed against the big plate-glass window and her bare hands red and rough with the cold.

I parked alongside and asked her what she thought she was doing there.

She ran over to the car. "I'm keeping the cat company," she told me. "He's in there all alone, and I was just telling him that the people will be back to-morrow, so he needn't be lonesome and scared."

Sure enough, the A&P cat was sitting in the window

rubbing his nose on the pane. To me he looked sleek and smug and perfectly satisfied with himself and the world; much more so, in fact, than my poor, worried child with her half frozen hands and grubby knees. I started to say so, a bit acidly, but I caught myself in time. What this world needs more than anything else is consideration and pity and love, and here I was about to blight a genuine demonstration of those qualities toward it didn't matter how un-needy and unworthy an object. Love and pity are never wasted. If I succeeded in hardening my daughter's heart to the supposed suffering of the A&P cat—or to the travail of an ant, shouldering his gigantic load, for that matter—how could I expect her to grow up to be the compassionate woman I wanted her to be?

So I said instead that I thought that was very thoughtful of her, and I was sure that the cat appreciated it, and that yes, she could run over and say good-bye to him.

The one who benefited chiefly by these trifling experiences was neither the cat, the mussels, Rufus, nor Dinah. It was Louise. It's too easy when you are busy and tired and worried to forget to be kind. I am not going to organize a Society for the Prevention of Cruelty to Shell-fish, nor am I going to set up a Trust Fund for the hiring of week-end baby-sitters for store cats. I shall probably continue upon occasion to say and do mean, thoughtless, cross-grained things, and in short to behave like the average adult, so-called. But I *hope* that once in a while, because I have been privileged to see what the human heart is like before it has grown its protective casing, I shall be able to do unconsidered, generous, childlike things. A child has nothing to give away except himself. As soon as we begin to possess other things, we lock ourselves away; and yet, in the end, our selves are the only things we have that are important and worth the giving. That is what my children have taught me.

When Dinah was four years old and Rufus was nine, at Christmas time I told them again the story of the Christ Child:—of the long, hard trip to Bethlehem, of the Inn that had no room, and of the Manger. It was the first year that Dinah had been old enough to understand. Her eyes filled with tears, and her chin quivered ominously.

"But Mummy," she said tightly, because even then it nearly killed her to cry in front of people, she was so proud, "Mummy, He'd be cold, and the cows and donkeys would look so big to Him, He'd be afraid."

I had forgotten that it was possible to feel concern—*real* concern—for the little Lord Jesus, asleep in the hay; but now I began to worry, too.

"Oh, no, He wouldn't, Dinah," Rufus told her, with never a pause for thought. "Gee whiz, His mother was there, wasn't she? She wouldn't let anything happen to Him. Ma doesn't let anything bad happen to us, does she?"

Dinah laughed in relief at her own foolish fears. " 'Course not. Go on, Mum. What happened next?"

For a minute I couldn't go on, so choked was I with humility and thanksgiving. When I did, my mind was only partly on the familiar story. I was thinking that Rufus' off-hand, spontaneous remark repaid me a hundred-fold for any inconvenience to which care for my children's welfare had put me.

That was six years ago, and I'm afraid that in those six years it has become apparent to my young that their mother is only human, an idol with feet of clay extending

Rufus rode us up the ten miles through the Narrows in his kicker-boat.

practically to the hip. She cannot avert tooth- or stomach-ache, nor command the rain to stop falling on a picnic or the sun to stand still in the sky; not effectively, at least. She bakes cakes that fall flat, and is powerless to prevent a sick pet from dying. She cannot even think of the right, healing things to say to render hurtless those dreadful wars of childhood, when the kid next door Isn't Speaking or is Having Secrets, and life is bitter and far from worth living. Oh, I know my short-comings as a parent! They are manifold. Those which I have failed to detect for myself have been pointed out to me by friends and relatives. Some of the charges launched against me I consider unjust; but I'm afraid that in the main the criticisms have been all too well founded. I am definitely a badly bent reed, when it comes to staving off either physical pain or heart-ache, and I know it. What I didn't know until yesterday was what the kids had found to take the place of their former blind belief in my omnipotence.

Day before yesterday—I am writing this at Forest Lodge—Dinah and her little guest, Janith Veinot, talked me into going with them up to Pine Island for over-night. We took food for supper and breakfast with us, and three sleeping bags. Rufus rode us up the ten miles through the Narrows in his kicker-boat, dumped us on the island, and left, not to return until noon the following day, yesterday. We were on our own.

We set up camp on the sandy beach, against a background of huge, sprawling pieces of dry-ki, lying like basking, pre-historic monsters against the edge of the forest. We swam, and cooked supper over a camp-fire, and then swam again. Finally we went to bed with nothing over us but the sky. We saw shooting stars and the Borealis and a plane going over; and we found the Big Dipper, and the Pole Star, and Cassiopeia's Chair. Then we went to sleep, and when we woke up the sun was just below the eastern horizon and the sky was full of pink feathers of clouds with gold edges. Birds flew all around us, busy and unafraid, and a deer came down on the opposite shore to drink. We got up and went swimming and had breakfast, and when Rufus arrived, were exploring the island. All in all, we had a wonderful time; but frankly—although I hate to admit this—I was looking forward to that night, when I could sleep in a bed.

The girls, however, were still full of enthusiasm. They wanted to go home and get enough food for two more days and nights, and then go right back to the island. Rufus became infected with the idea, and proposed that not only the girls, but he and his visiting friend Bruce and his tutor Frank join the expedition.

"Oh, no!" I screamed over the noise of the outboard. "I *can't!* I'm falling apart at the seams already. I can't take it another night so soon. Maybe later—"

He looked crest-fallen. "But Bruce is going home Tuesday."

"All right," I compromised. "You can all go if Frank is willing to go with you, and you all promise to obey him."

Both kids immediately put up a howl. "We want you to come, too!"

"That's perfectly ridiculous," I told them shortly. "You're both old enough to look after yourselves, and if you aren't, Frank is quite capable of looking after you. There's no need of my going at all."

They received this pronouncement in stony silence.

"Is there?" I demanded.

"Well, no," Rufus admitted reluctantly. Then he added vociferously, "But gee, Ma, you don't *understand.* Things are more fun with you!"

If you're not a parent yourself, you don't know how I felt, and I can't possibly tell you.

All I can say is that I'm a darn fortunate woman.

THE END